MORE RELAXING, LESS TAXING

MORE RELAXING, LESS TAXING

*Why You Would Be Brain
Dead Not to Own a Business*

COURTNEY EPPS

Clovercroft Publishing

More Relaxing, Less Taxing

©2019 by Courtney Epps

Published by Clovercroft Publishing, Franklin, Tennessee

Edited by Robert Irvin

Cover Design by Adept Content Solutions

Interior Design by Suzanne Lawing

Printed in the United States of America

ISBN: 978-1-948484-50-3

CONTENTS

ABOUT THE AUTHOR
AND THIS BOOK

Courtney Epps is the CEO for her company, Outside the Box Business Solutions, LLC, which is a consulting and full-service accounting firm. She is a Fractional CFO for dozens of small to mid-size companies nationwide. Courtney has been in the accounting and finance industry for eighteen years. She graduated from Coastal Carolina University in 2002. She has owned and worked in numerous companies in many industries including retail, advertising agencies, home-based businesses, network marketing companies, apparel, and fundraising; her largest company was an insurance agency in Myrtle Beach with close to three thousand, five hundred clients. She has done accounting for businesses exceeding $50 million in sales, and her largest CFO client at the time of this book's publication is a $13 million business.

Courtney's passion is to help individuals, home-based businesses, and brick and mortar businesses become educated in saving money on taxes legally, morally, and ethically. Courtney's specialty is finding and saving money that companies and individuals did not know existed.

This book will teach you:

• Why you must have a business.

• What deductions are crucial to your business that your

accountant/bookkeeper may be missing.

- How to make your business more profitable without increasing sales.

- Why most self-employed people are giving away an extra $10,000 to $20,000 annually to the IRS, and how you can get every deduction you are legally entitled to receive.

- Why everyone should have a business, whether home-based or traditional, in today's economy. This will help with massive tax savings.

- How you can legally pay for your kids' hobbies, birthdays, and college, and your car, through your business—tax free.

- Fringe benefits you can offer that will save you thousands in tax deductions to write off medical bills, gym memberships, and day care without limits.

- How you can write off your fun, including meals, entertainment, and travel.

- Also, how to double your deductions for some of these items, and to do so with the IRS's blessings.

- We will also discuss a way to write off almost any meal.

- How not writing off your home office can cost you, easily, $5,000 per year.

- Extra ways to squeeze a ton of money from your tax return—and all legally.

- How to audit-proof yourself.

PREFACE

This book should be read before tax season. First, your accountant is stressed and overworked during tax season. He or she doesn't have time to review your business and find deductions that you have not been writing off. So here's the first piece of advice I have for you: get ahead of the game and start discussing the principles of this book now with your tax strategist to put in place a plan to save you money! If you wait until tax season, you will not receive the time and attention you need, and the prior year will be over, not allowing you to obtain the write-offs you are legally entitled to.

I want to be clear that if your accountant, CPA, or EA tells you that you cannot do the things found in this book, then you have the wrong accountant! This book is straight by the Internal Revenue Service (IRS) tax code. You also cannot depend on your accountant to do this for you, as that is usually not their role. The role of a typical firm is to prepare your tax return, and that is what you are paying them for.

There is huge difference between *tax preparation* and

tax planning. This book will walk you through why tax planning should be the most important thing you implement in your business. If not, you are giving away your money.

I would like to thank my family. First of all, my husband, Brandon, who has stood beside me through it all. My children, Alexis, Adrianne, Sawyer, Wells, Cooper, and Lilli. They are my inspiration to continue working harder daily. My parents, Jan and Willie West, who taught me to have an amazing work ethic and never give up. This book is a collection of the eighteen years I have spent running and owning businesses. I have learned a great deal through what Keith Cunningham calls the "dumb tax," or trial and error. In business, I have made and lost hundreds of thousands of dollars. I have been through every trial and tribulation one can imagine, and I definitely felt like quitting many times. I have had employees steal from me, lost a business, had to go out of business and start over from scratch.

I did not learn the information I am teaching in this book in college. It was through my own mission to save money and help my clients that I learned the tax strategies that I know and teach today. Most accountants simply don't know the information that you will learn here because they did not dive deeper into their education, as I did.

I know this book with save you so much money if you utilize the information in it, and it will open your eyes to a world that is *More Relaxing, Less Taxing.*

—Courtney Epps

CHAPTER 1

Why You Must Have a Business

If you're an entrepreneur you have heard the million reasons not to go into business: it's too risky, you might go into debt, you'll probably lose sleep, you will not have a social life, and the list goes on. I am going to share with you why you *should* get in business for yourself, and why it is the single most important decision you will make in your life—and why. Now, what I am not saying is to leave your job or career and "get into business." What I am saying is that every person needs a business and that every business owner with a traditional business should have some type of home-based business. Warren Buffett says, "Never depend on one income. Make an investment to create a second source."[1]

Did you know that the average household income in this country is $61,000? That typical household then pays $12,000 in taxes, leaving that family about $49,000 to live on. The sad truth is that the average cost of living in

America is $53,000, leaving families further and further in debt, to the tune of a whopping $4,000 per year. Now if you knew that you were going to work forty hours a week for fifty-two weeks a year and that you would owe more when the fifty-two weeks were up than you did today, would you still head in to work? This is the cold, hard truth, but there is a way to fix it.

And the way to fix it is by taking advantage of the second tax system we have in this country.

There are two tax systems in this country—one for salaried employees, and one for small/home-based business owners. By having a business, you have more tax deductions, allowing you to pay less in taxes, and this book will teach you how to do that. On average, I see savings of $4,000 to $8,000 per year in taxes by starting your own part-time home-based business. Understand: *if you do not get your taxes down to the legal minimum, you will never be able to maximize your income potential.* If you have a traditional business with a location away from your home, I see thousands of dollars going down the drain each year for you because of a lack of tax planning.

There are numerous other reasons why you want to own a business. These include pride of ownership.

There are numerous other reasons why you want to own a business. These include pride of ownership. There is a certain level of pride involved with something that you built, of which you can say, "I did this." Instead of building someone else's income or dream, you could be building for your retirement, vacations, and dream homes or cars. There is also a level of pride that your spouse, children, family, and friends have for you that might even feel better than the pride you could have for yourself.

Building a brand for your business is not only fun, it gives you another level of satisfaction—that you have created something bigger than yourself. Also, as you develop your business and your brand, your expertise in that field continues to get greater, allowing you to not only make more at what you are doing, but also providing you opportunities to speak and get paid to share what you know in your industry. The more you learn in business, the more you earn. That is not necessarily the case in standard education.

A lot of people begin their own business so they will have more free time. The reason some quit is that they find out, at some point, that you have to work for a long time to achieve that free time. Why? Because you have to build your business in the beginning. Once you have all the systems and people in place, then the business can start building itself, allowing you to have more time to do the things you want to do on your terms, not doing them only when your boss tells you. The thing I enjoy most about having a business is that I can work when I want to work—but I *must* work. Understand that. If I want to take the day off to spend time with my kids, I can. You just have to realize that if you continue to do that and don't make up the work you missed or leverage someone else to do it, you will not be in business very long.

One of the greatest reasons to build a company is to one day leave a legacy for your family. The empire must be built by both you and them together. No matter how hard you work at a job, your children cannot inherit it. Knowing what I know about the job market and the fact that my children would be giving up 40 percent of their income in taxes—well, this just makes me sick. It is incentive for me to want to build a big enough company so they have options in life. And what about the next generation? I do not know if it will be any better for them. Wouldn't it be a great feeling to know that you single-handedly started a business that set your family free for life? Now, I am not saying that they should not work for what they earn, because I believe you must work hard or smart—and often you have to do both to get ahead in the beginning.

Now, a big reason to own your business is that job security is drastically declining and millennials are replacing baby boomers every day in jobs. With the advent of massive technology, the things we went to school for become more and more obsolete—and this could leave you without a job. People are being replaced with computers and kiosks in restaurants and other businesses on a daily basis. By owning your business, you learn a set of skills that can be used to change the products or services you offer and allow you to start something completely new. When you learn the skills, you can do anything you want in business. And even if one business fails, you can start all over.

Giving back is another amazing part of owning a business. This concept allows you to be able to give back to the community in ways you never would have thought possible, whether through time or money. A growing

Giving back is another amazing part of owning a business. This concept allows you to be able to give back to the community in ways you never would have thought possible .

concept in our society now is something called social giving, and this empowers your network to give on a larger scale. It is a wonderful concept, and you will learn more about this in Chapter 12 of this book. You will also learn that a "buy one–give one" model is one of the greatest ways to not only help a charity that you love but also one that ties in your profits with purpose and saves your tax dollars along the way so you can give more. Practicing these things will escalate your business at a level you could not imagine.

Another great thing about running your own business is that things are constantly changing. Sometimes they change for the worse and sometimes for the better, but you can never say that running your own business is boring. It is more like a roller coaster ride. Working for someone and doing the same thing over and over again makes for a very boring life.

A great part of business is the people you meet along the way. Your clients become your greatest friends because you have common traits and goals. Hopefully, your employees are on a path with you to change the world—if that is one of your goals. Through networking you meet people you can pass referrals to, and they can pass back to you. You also have people you can pass ideas by, receiving suggestions on how to make your business more successful. Then, when you face a crisis or things are not going as planned, you have people you can reach out to, who can help you through the bad times, because they understand the bad times only stay for a little while. This will help you come to grips with your emotions and keep you from making poor decisions.

The need for continuing education in business is crucial. If you are not growing, you will die in business. You can learn from some of the most amazing leaders you can imagine. I tend to follow Tony Robbins, Les Brown, Steve Harvey, Jim Rohn, Zig Ziglar, John Maxwell, Eric Worre, and Grant Cardone—all of these provide fantastic teachings about business. Although Ziglar and Rohn are not with us today, I still rely on the things I've learned from them through events, videos, and books. Here's one of those things: you must realize that you are the average of the top five people you spend time with. If you are the most successful person in your group, you may want to find another group of people to hang out with as well, or choose to go to some events to spend time with

My business has grown ten times from the information I've learned from other leaders.

people who can help you grow you as a person and business owner and get you more excited and strategic about your business. I can tell you specific things I learned at certain events put me on another path, one I would not have traveled without the new information I learned. My business has grown exponentially from the information I've learned from other leaders.

The business skills you learn are like no other. These skills are taught through true immersion. As there are so many moving parts in business, there are definitely things you do not know how to do, that you are either going to learn through advice from consultants, YouTube videos, competitors, or trusted business advisors. Some of these skills are learned through trial and error and will cost you a lot of money simply because you don't yet know them! Some mistakes cost a lot more time and money than others, but the skills you learn in business can be moved to the next business, and the education is truly priceless. Your failures will become your greatest learning moments if you allow them to be.

Mentoring people who lack the education you have is not only a great way to give back but also is one of the most rewarding things you will experience in your business if you allow it to happen. You can take someone under your wing and share valuable skills they can use to make their life better.

The sheer will and determination of some entrepreneurs at times amazes me. Business owners see light at the end of a tunnel that no one else sees. They have a bigger vision, one the average person tends to overlook. The determination to continue when everything looks bleak is a great asset in business, and if you obtain that skill, it will affect every part of your life. I used to give up before I finished anything. Then I realized there are so many things worth finishing—like this book, like a diet and exercise plan, like a better life for my family. Business forces you to realize that although times get hard, they will not stay that way. There is a season for everything, and business owners know all too well what that means. The determination to be a business owner has made me a better wife, mother, friend, and employer because I realize you can't give up when things look bad or when you fail. If you do, you will always be a failure. You should at least give yourself another chance to be a success. I have failed and succeeded in business numerous times. I had to pick myself up, dust myself off, and keep going for my family and everyone else who depended on me.

Creating jobs is imperative for our economy because not everyone wants to become an entrepreneur and run their own business. Your ideas and business will not only change your life but hugely impact the lives of others. It feels great knowing you are not only providing for your family, you are also providing support for other people through employment. Also, Congress allows for some massive tax deductions because of this principle, and we will talk more about these later in the book.

As you continue to get better at what you do in business, opportunities come your way that you would not otherwise have known about—or had access to. This allows, if you want, the chance to constantly transform or reinvent yourself to be and do what you want to do, not what you have to do. As an entrepreneur, you can be whatever you want—as opposed to, believe it or not, being a doctor or lawyer. Also, you can start a new business or service tomorrow if you get bored with what you're doing, and it doesn't have to cost you a lot of money or years in education to do so.

The recognition you receive from building and owning a successful business is priceless. You may receive awards from the local chamber of commerce—or maybe climb the scale as high as winning a Nobel prize. Muhammad Yunus won a Nobel prize for creating social business, but he has also affected the lives of more than 40 million people by creating The Grameen Bank in Bangladesh. This bank provides microloans to families to help them start their own businesses, allowing them a choice of whether they will live in poverty or not. Unas won true recognition, but more important, his actions helped change the world at the same time. You can read about the impact he has made in his book *Building Social Business*.

You may say that every business owner thinks they are going to change the world, but your service or business may not be life-changing. Take a look at these people: Walt Disney, the Rockefellers, Sam Walton, Bill Gates, Steve Jobs, Tony Robbins. All had visions of what they wanted to do for themselves and their families. While they were building their businesses, they just so happened to inspire people, change the world as we know it, and carry a lot of people along the way. Eventually, each of these people ended up with less of a business and more of an empire! So, even if you think your idea is not a big deal, do not sell yourself short. We tend to overestimate what we can do in one year but drastically underestimate what we can do in five to ten years. Start something now that is life-changing for

> *We tend to overestimate what we can do in one year but drastically underestimate what we can do in five to ten years.*

you, your family, and everyone surrounding you . . . from now to ten years from now. You only have one life to live.

One of the chief reasons people get involved in business is they want time and money freedom. The problem with this is they give up way too soon to receive either. Financial independence is a big deal, and that is why people are willing to work on an underpaid basis for thirty years of their life, because they think their pension—and these are now almost extinct—or 401k are going to get them through their retirement years. The sad truth is that most people will outlive the money they have set aside not because they planned to fail but because they failed to plan. They were not taught financial freedom in school, and they leave their money to be managed by people who don't even know them. (These are commonly called fund managers.) Wealthy people realize that 401k's, jobs, CDs, and IRAs are not going to make them wealthy. They work on another level. The first principle is they pay the legal minimum in taxes. You must understand this: wealthy people have figured out ways to make more money through leveraging other people's time and/or money—all while paying less in taxes.

This book will show you how to pay less in taxes so you can be on a road to financial freedom. But you must first take the leap of faith and become an entrepreneur. Once again, I am not telling you to quit your day job. I am telling you to find something you are passionate about and start a business around it on a part-time basis so you can achieve the greatest tax savings possible.

TYPES OF BUSINESSES TO START

Direct Sales, Affiliate Marketing, or Network Marketing

You may want to find a direct sales or network marketing company. These companies are reasonably priced and allow you to begin on a part-time basis. Direct sales has not only given me some of the greatest friends, it's also given me some amazing business partners. On top of that, it's given me the personal and business development I so desperately need and would not have found anywhere else. Indirectly, it quadrupled my accounting practice! I work with numerous leaders in the industry, helping them do three things: attract, retain, and grow their customer base and teams. But please understand that you can't just sign up in a company and expect tax deductions; you have to attempt to earn an income. The best way to show the IRS you are making every effort to do this is sharing the company and products with your friends and family. A little-known secret is attending training events and subscribing to the tools offered for tax savings. Education is power, but it also lets the IRS know you are truly treating this as a business—and that you intend to make money. It allows you to turn some of your vacation costs into tax deductible business expenses.

If you will do these two

The average American pays more in taxes than he or she does on food, housing, transportation, and clothing combined!

simple things, you are well on your way: share and utilize events and tools. In doing so, not only will your income increase drastically over time, you can also cut your personal expenses, including Internet, telephone, business use of your home, vehicles, meals, and hundreds of other expenses—these *can all be tax deductible*, leaving you with more money in your pocket, or to put back into your business. If you are an employee of a business, taxes are your greatest expense. The average American pays more in taxes than he or she does on food, housing, transportation, and clothing combined! A new business opportunity is the vehicle that will help you increase income and lower your taxes at the same time. And because of it, you are now on the quickest path to building wealth.

The downside of owning such a company is you may not be interested in sales. Nonetheless, you must understand that you are always selling. It may be you that is being sold, or a product, but sales are going to continue to happen. If sales are something you are passionate about, you are already on the right foot, and you won't have to be concerned about whether you can make it in this area. If you do not have a sales background, that is great. The leaders in the industry will teach you quickly that it is not about selling anything. It is all about sharing something that you are passionate about and getting paid for it. Even if you are the worst salesperson, you can make it in this industry because your passion will shine through if you are trying to help someone. Just by sharing, you are entitled to many tax deductions on money that you are already spending. So if you sit down with your friend and share with them a product or service that you are excited about and they tell you no, it is OK. They just do not understand that not only are you trying to help them, you are also getting massive tax deductions to do so. Your friend has not been properly educated, and it is costing them money. You are the smart one.

Franchise Businesses

The great thing about a franchise business is the business is already established; you already have a trusted brand and product. The downside is you are going to pay to for it. There are two things you will learn in business quickly. You will either pay with your money, or your sweat equity, to create a successful business. Because someone else has already done this and put in both of those things, you are going to have to pay more to be a part of what they have built, as opposed to starting your own business or being in direct sales. This type of business, however, does provide you with a team of support that you won't typically get in traditional business. Unlike Direct Sales, where you do not pay for it, you will pay heavily for it here. On the other hand, because it is an established business and brand, your chances of success could be far greater than the traditional approach.

Traditional, Brick and Mortar, or Home-Based Businesses

A traditional business, depending on what type you decide to get involved in, could cost anywhere from a couple of hundred dollars to hundreds of thousands of dollars to start. Most people, when they think of traditional business, believe you are talking about an actual office or commercial space, and with employees. We call these brick and mortar businesses. A traditional business is a business that is started from scratch with products or services—whether it has a commercial location or not. For example, I had a commercial space for many of the eighteen years of my business life. What I realized was I could redirect a lot of my personal expenses into business expenses if I had my accounting practice at home, and I could save thousands of dollars a month in office space and utility bills by having a home-based business. While I have tons of clients that are brick and mortar, I also have hundreds of clients who are operating their businesses, like me, out of their homes. Now, if I had clients coming to see me every day, it may be necessary to have an office offsite. But it is not, and my family has made the home-based business work really well with our family life. Our employees come here to work, and I meet most of our clients at their brick and mortar locations. Everything else is handled through the Internet, e-mail, or social media.

Regardless of what type of business you decide to begin, you need to start one immediately. In the next few chapters, you will learn what the majority of business owners don't understand, and what you need to know to not only be successful in business but also save the most money in taxes you can. This will allow you to build your business and get closer to the path of financial freedom.

To be able to do that, the first step is understanding the difference between tax preparation and tax planning.

CHAPTER 2

Tax Preparation Versus Tax Planning
(What you don't know is costing you thousands of dollars a year—or more!)

As taxes can take up as much as 50 percent of your income, tax planning is one of the most important investments you can make.
—COURTNEY EPPS

I have proven that most self-employed people, even when using a good accountant, overpay, on average, about $7,000 or more per year in taxes per $100,000 in sales. This is a *huge* amount of money for a small- to medium-sized business. If you add that up over ten or more years, that could be hundreds of thousands of dollars that could have been used to put back into your business or pay off a mortgage, place in a retirement account, or pay for college for your kids.

Every day I run into clients who are trying to cut costs with their businesses. The problem is they are cutting costs on some of the most important aspects of the business, things like marketing, payroll, and accounting, when they should be investing in tax planning and cost accounting so they can save on their biggest expense: taxes. I find that small companies usually get started and are strapped for cash in their early days. These owners are trying to grow a business on a very small budget. Small companies tend to try to handle the accounting on their own, and then, later, hire an office manager/bookkeeper to handle the books. The bad part about this is the owner usually has no time to check up on the work of the bookkeeper, and as long as the sales—and bills—are still coming in, no one is taking a close look at what is being done.

I am not saying the bookkeeper is, in any way, failing to do his or her job, but I have found that what a business owner thinks a bookkeeper is supposed to do and what that person actually does are usually two different things. A bookkeeper's role is to input data and handle accounts payable and accounts receivable. This person is there to pay your bills and collect money from your clients. Thus, bookkeepers usually have no understanding of financial statements and what they need to do to help you save money. Also, there is a payroll company involved, usually, and its only job is to make sure that your payroll is paid, taxes are paid, and payroll filings are taken care of. Then there is the tax accountant or CPA. This is the person the business owner puts his or her most faith and trust in, banking that this person will save them money, especially in taxes. But the tax accountant, usually, is the person spending the least time looking at the numbers. Also, by the time the accountant gets the information to prepare your return, the year is already up, and there is not much that can be done at that point to save money on taxes.

Then comes the business coach or consultant. This person is trying to help you run your company based on the numbers given to him or her by three different resources: the bookkeeper, tax accountant, and payroll company. And guess what? All of these people are usually talking to the business owner—but they are not talking to each other. And insurance brokers rely on numbers that may or may not be correct for insurance premiums. Any or all of these issues could cause your business to fall apart. Your finances are the most crucial part of your company, and they are being left to numerous people who only have parts of the puzzle. In Chapter 4 I will teach you that if you want a clearer picture of your business, a Fractional CFO is crucial, and this person will save you more money in your business than what he or she will cost.

> *The sad truth is that out of all these people, none are helping you save money in taxes, because that is not what you hired them to do—nor is it their expertise.*

The sad truth is that out of all these people, none are helping you save money in taxes, because that is not what you hired them to do—nor is it their expertise. In the five years of study I underwent in college, there was not a single class on "How to Save Your Clients Money." If there had been, I would have taken it! The classes offered dealt with how to prepare good books for tax preparation and how to prepare good financials to help with cost accounting.

So, what is the difference between tax preparation and tax planning? Tax preparation deals with income and numbers from the past. It is what has to be done to get the filing completed so you can get your tax returns finished. Meanwhile, tax planning determines ways to minimize the amount of taxes a client has to pay.

Now, you may be saying to yourself that tax planning is not important because you didn't make a lot of money this year. This could not be further from the truth. The last great tax shelter left in this country is for the home-based business and small business owner. Also, if your deductions exceed your income, then you are able to take those losses, dollar for dollar, against any income you have.

Example: Jim earned $75,000 in salary. His wife Sally is in a home-based business, and it generated a loss of $18,000. This loss would be deducted from Jim's salary, leaving them $57,000 net income on which to pay taxes.

So what happens if you have more expenses than you do income in one year? The IRS allows something called a Net Operating Loss (NOL) Carryforward, and it allows you to take the losses to deduct against any earnings in the future.

Example: Sally has a loss of $20,000 from her business from a prior year and $10,000 in losses this year. Jim and Sally would only pay taxes on $45,000 of Jim's $75,000 salary because of the carryforward. This would save more than $10,000 in taxes.

As you can see, tax planning strategy is hugely important regardless of how much money you make. In a great book, *The Millionaire Next Door: The Surprising Secrets of America's Wealthy,* authors Thomas Stanley and William Danko analyzed the similarities of multimillionaires and their mind-sets. The rich believe that, to get rich, you have to get your taxes down to the legal minimum. In other words, you need to understand the rules of the tax game. The wealthy don't pay less in taxes because they are rich. They are rich because they pay less in taxes. The rich understand

The wealthy don't pay less in taxes because they are rich. They are rich because they pay less in taxes.

the two different tax systems we have in this country, and those two systems are *not* one for the rich and one for the poor. There is one that is for employees, and it is designed to take your wealth away. The second system is for the self-employed, and that system is designed to help you create more wealth and create economic growth in our country. The government knows that more jobs are created by small and home-based businesses than large corporations. Because of this, Congress has passed some great tax laws for small businesses, and you should make it your business to know these laws to achieve greater tax savings.

The authors of *The Millionaire Next Door* show that most people who became millionaires were average people who saved money each year and invested that money for thirty or more years. Now, you may be saying to yourself that you do not have extra money to invest! That is why you must understand that tax planning is so crucial and can allow you to keep more of your money so you can become wealthy one day as well.

Throughout my eighteen years as an accountant, so many people have told me that their accountant takes care of their taxes, or perhaps that their bookkeeper handles that responsibility. The problem with this is your bookkeeper usually does not *know* taxes; and your accountant or tax preparer is getting your tax documents, most often, in January or February. That person then begins doing your taxes along with about two hundred to three hundred other returns! This leaves them roughly two to three hours to deal with your return. The other problem is that if the information is not getting to them until the new year, minimal tax planning strategies are going to be able to be used for the *previous* year. This is like saying that if you sign up for a gym membership, that alone will take care of your weight and health. The truth is, if you do not regularly utilize that membership, it does you no good. The same holds true for your taxes. If you are not utilizing your accountant or a tax strategist outside of tax

If you are not utilizing your accountant or a tax strategist outside of tax season for tax planning, it will cost you a lot more in taxes than you could ever pay for the service!

season for tax planning, it will cost you a lot more in taxes than you could ever pay for the service! Also, understand this: not all accountants are created equal. If you put ten different accountants in a room with the same tax information, you will typically come away with ten different tax returns. Why? Because it depends on the accountant's view of the tax code, and also their knowledge. If your accountant tells you that you can't write off a business because you have not made a profit, run! Why? Because almost all businesses have a loss for the first couple of years as the owner or owners are growing and funding the company with their own money. Such poor advice would be like telling Chrysler and Ford that they could not claim losses in 2008 and 2009 when almost every area of the auto industry similarly was taking a huge hit. So, know this principle: if something does not make sense for a big business, more than likely small businesses have the same tax benefits, and it would not make sense for small business owners to miss such deductions either.

Also, if your accountant tells you that you should not write off certain things because it could trigger an audit, I would find another accountant. This person is not going to help you save money, and this advice will cost you so much in the long run.

Of course, understand that you have to be in business for the main purpose of earning an income. You cannot just join a network marketing or home-based business company because you want tax write-offs or products at wholesale and to be able to claim this as a business. The IRS states that a tax-deductible business expense is any expense that is incurred for the purpose of gaining or producing income and incurred with a reasonable expectation of resulting in future business and is reasonable under the circumstances. What does this mean? If you are attempting to earn an income, whether you do or not, you are deemed to be in business and therefore entitled to business deductions.

I will show you numerous tax deductions throughout this book that I did not know existed while I was going through school; we were not taught to save money for our clients or ourselves. I learned these things through my own research, from books by other experts, and from the IRS tax code, publications, and letter rulings.

Next, we will explore the difference between cost accounting and tax accounting, and why you must know both to win in running your business.

CHAPTER 3

Cost Accounting Versus Tax Accounting

One thing many clients have no understanding of is that there is a huge difference between cost accounting and tax accounting. Even though a bookkeeper is doing day-to-day operations and accountants are handling taxes, often a lack of communication and a hands-off approach by the business owner causes the business to drastically overpay, or pay for things it should not have to. If you are not being asked questions like these: "Why are you spending money on these items?"; "Why has this gone up in price?"; "Why are you paying so much in interest or merchant fees?"—then you are losing money. Lack of communication also may cause a business owner to be paying two people to do the same thing, including data entry. Understand that the bookkeeper and the accountant are just keeping track of all (well, hopefully all) of the financial information, and making sure that the business is moving in the right direction. Saving money is not at the forefront of their minds, so as a business owner it has to be your highest priority so you can maximize your bottom line and make sure you stay in business in the beginning.

In wanting to be proactive to figure out how to make more income, you may hire a consultant or coach in the hope that they will provide sound advice on growing your business. The problem with this is the consultant is not collaborating with your team, only you. So, ultimately, you are looking at paying your bookkeeper and your accountant (usually around $150 an hour) to explain what you learned from the consultant and what needs to be done moving forward. So, on top of your already packed schedule, you now have more work to do. Another issue is that your consultant may not be looking to diagnose your big and small cash-leak issues. In their eyes, as long as they are helping increase your company's profitability, they've successfully done their jobs. Yet, what good is it to provide increases if the cash flow leaks have not been diagnosed and fixed? If your expenses increase at the same rate of income, what is the point of "making more money"? That's just more work for no more pay.

> *Another issue is that your consultant may not be looking to diagnose your big and small cash-leak issues.*

Experts and employees aside, perhaps you have tried implementing solutions of your own for what you think is causing your cash flow problem. You may think you simply need to work harder and longer hours. All that will result in is increased stress and less time to do what you want or love. Maybe if you spend a little more for advertising, or spruce up your website and increase your social media presence, more customers will come and inject more money into your business. While all these steps are wise marketing moves, how do you know how much they will pay off down the road if you can't read—or don't have—financial documents to show you the effects?

Before jumping into all these extra investments of time and money, why not start with a more simplistic and productive approach that will have maximum impact on your bottom line? After all, didn't you originally become your own boss to avoid working long hours, being short on cash, and facing stress all the time? What you really need, first and foremost, is someone willing to roll up their sleeves and find the cash flow leaks, then give you a practical plan to fix them and prevent future ones, thus saving you time and money.

These leaks are always at least partly due to taxes—and there are usually thousands of dollars of other expenses as well that could be costing your business. You must have the correct tools—and optics—to see the problems and know how to fix them if you want to survive in business.

CHAPTER 4

Having a Clearer Vision of Your Business and Why a Fractional CFO Is Crucial

As an owner of a privately held company, you are constantly faced with challenges: optimizing cash flow, maximizing profitability, accelerating growth, and planning your exit strategies. Fractional CFOs partner with you to develop a game plan for the myriad of strategic, financial, and business challenges you face. Because a Fractional CFO is outside your business looking in, he or she tends to see issues that would not otherwise be caught. This person can provide the expertise needed to perform critical financial officer duties on a consulting or part-time basis. Fractional CFOs carefully listen to your goals, aspirations, challenges, and frustrations and help fix problems. They are a partner in a real sense. They allow you to benefit from their expertise without having to come out of pocket for the cost of a full-time CFO salary. They also provide another level of accountability and make sure your team is on the right track and doing what it takes to not only save money but maximize profits.

These are some of the critical benefits I've found from a Fractional CFO. We all know that cash flow is the life-blood of a business. If you do not have enough cash flow, your business will not make it for long. Your business may be just starting up, or you are making lots of money, but where is the money going? What are your profit margins? How are you doing compared to your budget—if you even have a budget! What are your prior year comparisons? Are you increasing sales but at the same time increasing expenses as well?

A Fractional CFO's mission is to help businesses like yours save money by combing through all of your book-keeper's and accountant's work to look at every aspect of your business and determine where they can save you money. Often, when you find yourself in a financial situation and must find ways to save money, your advisors may tell you to cut costs or downsize. But a Fractional CFO will dig deeper and work with your financial staff to instill smart processes to help save time and money without hurting your business along the way. In fact, their goal is to help get you out of a scarcity mentality and increase your income. For example, you may be worried that you don't have enough to pay the bills, or you may be anxious about what you'll owe

> *Their goal is to help get you out of a scarcity mentality and increase your income.*

in taxes. These things are putting a cap on your income. A Fractional CFO gives you a handle so you know how much you owe and where your finances are in terms of how much money is coming in and how much is going out. He or she will also help you decrease your business expenses everywhere they can, and help you maximize tax deductions to make sure you are paying the least amount possible—all while helping you have all the coverage and services you need. Once you understand how much money you have to work with, the scarcity mentality flies away, and you can do the right things to focus on making more money.

But perhaps the biggest area in which a Fractional CFO can help is to uncover your nest egg of savings in taxes once systems and strategies are in place. Throughout the year, you may think you made a lot of money—until tax time comes, and you find yourself paying 40 to 50 percent of your hard-earned money to the government. *Forbes* says that about 95 percent of all businesses overpay in taxes. And this can be the case even with a great bookkeeper, accountant, payroll company, and coach/consultant—all because the company failed on the tax planning and strategy portion of the business. And this is the part that you do not want to overlook; if you do, it will cost you the most.

As we continue, I'm going to teach you some of the strategies and tax deductions you

Learn how to keep more of your money—so your life can be more relaxing and less taxing.

and your financial team are possibly missing. Do not leave tens of thousands of dollars on the table each year. Learn how to keep more of your money—whether you do or do not have a Fractional CFO—so your life can be more relaxing and less taxing.

Do note this: if your company is bringing in between $500,000 and $5 million, it is crucial you hire a Fractional CFO today; this is a company that is too big to handle on your own. You can't run the books and run the business at the same time.

CHAPTER 5

Commonly Missed Tax Deductions

Cutting back on taxes is the number one move that will put more money in your pocket, and it is the fastest and easiest way to do so. Through this book, I want to stop you from giving away all of those extra hundreds and thousands of dollars and show you how you can get every deduction you are legally entitled to receive.

The first step is to look at deductions you are not currently using or deductions that are slipping through the cracks. Your accountant and bookkeeper are not looking for them, and there will be no paper trail because some key expenses may be from a personal bank account or credit card that is not being tracked on the books.

I recently amended three years' worth of returns for a client who overpaid about $47,000 in taxes because her bookkeeper and accountant did not track her personal credit cards she was using for business expenses. That's

. . . crazy. This chapter will teach you about some deductions you have never heard of and some your accountant has said you can't write off. I want to change such patterns for you today.

This chapter will teach you about some deductions you have never heard of and some your accountant has said you can't write off.

There are so many proactive ways to keep more of your hard-earned money where it belongs: with you. For instance, you can legally pay your kids and they can pay for college, weddings, cars, and more through your business—tax free. There are tips on how you can write off more of your fun, including meals and travel. Did you know there is a trick to write off your equipment, like cars, computers, and office furniture, and do so twice? Did you know about hiring your spouse and being able to write off all your medical bills and numerous other expenses as a fringe benefit through your business, and in which you will not be subject to Adjusted Gross Income restrictions?

START-UP COSTS

If you are in your first year of business, costs you incurred before you began operations are deductible, up to $5,000. And if you spent more than $5,000, the costs are amortized over time.

Home Office Deduction

Quickbooks estimates that only about 33 percent of all self-employed individuals claim a home office deduction. Many people avoid taking this obvious deduction because there are a lot of catches to it, and they think using it can trigger an audit. In reality, the IRS applies a simple two-part test:

Many people avoid taking this obvious deduction because there are a lot of catches to it, and they think using it can trigger an audit.

- One, the dedicated space in your home must be used as your principle place of business, or it must have some other acceptable business purpose.

- Two, it must be used regularly and exclusively for the business.

If you meet these criteria, then the applicable percentage of homeowners insurance, mortgage interest or rent, repairs and maintenance, utility bills, and more can be deducted.

Here's how this works: if your kitchen table doubles as your work desk, you cannot deduct it. However, if you have a dedicated room, or even a portion of a room, you can deduct some of your housing costs.

Example: The business owner uses 10 percent of his home for an office.

	Expense	Home Office Percent	Deduction
Mortgage interest	$10,485	10%	$1,048.50
Real estate property tax	$1,800	10%	$180.00
Utilities	$3,975	10%	$397.50
Homeowners insurance	$1,500	10%	$150.00
Alarm system	$720	10%	$72.00
Home office repairs	$1,850	10%	$185.00
Depreciation of home	$2,500	10%	$250.00
Depreciation of furniture	$750	10%	$75.00
Tax Deductions			**$2,358.00**

Auto Expenses

If you travel to meet a client, perform a job outside your business, purchase business supplies, conduct research, or do any other kind of activity for your business, you can deduct these expenses. You have the option to write off the actual mileage based on your business use percentage including gas, oil changes, car washes, maintenance and repairs, and depreciation, or you can take the standard mileage deductions.

But with the new tax law changes passed in 2017, it is almost never a good idea to take the standard mileage method.

Healthcare Insurance Premiums

This is a deduction that is simply not available to employees. In most cases, because you are self-employed, you buy your own medical insurance. If this is the case, you can deduct 100 percent of what it costs to cover yourself and your family. This includes Medicare premiums. But there is a big exception for the self-employed. You can deduct what you pay for medical insurance for yourself and your family whether you itemize or not. This allows you to take a 100 percent deduction with no regard to the 7.5 percent threshold. You do not qualify if you are eligible for employer-sponsored health insurance through your job, if you are covered by a plan in addition to your business, or covered through a spouse's job.

Retirement Plans

This is one of the most profitable deductions of all for the self-employed. Unlike employees, whose options are limited to whatever their employer offers, and putting up to $5,500 in an IRA each year, business owners can contribute pretax money to a simplified employee pension (SEP) or a solo 401k as well as the IRA. Your contributions to IRAs and 401k plans benefit you in two ways: The first is that you can make annual salary deferrals of up to $18,500 and 25 percent of net income in 2018 plus an additional $6,000 if you're 50 or older and it is tax deductible. Even better, you can contribute as much as 25 percent of your net earnings from self-employment (not including contributions for yourself), up to $55,000. The second is that, because the money is tax-deferred, the government is rewarding you for creating your own retirement plan by not taxing you on the income until you withdraw the money further down the road.

Interest Payments

I constantly see that this is a huge missed tax deduction. From finance charges on a credit card to interest payments for vehicles, equipment, and loans—these things can be deducted. Business owners traditionally start operating with personal bank accounts, loans, and credit cards and tend to forget to write off those interest charges.

Capital Expenditures

When you buy large items for your business (e.g., autos, computer systems, and more), you have two choices on how to deduct the costs. The first is to depreciate the cost, deducting the expenses over a number of years, considered the "life" of the equipment or property. Depending on the situation, especially at the beginning of your business, where you may have losses, you have the option of writing off the equipment or property over multiple years, and this could possibly save you a great deal in years to come. The second way is to expense the property or equipment using a Section 179 deduction. This allows you to deduct 100 percent of the qualifying cost up to your net income in the first year. In 2018, the new tax code increased the Section 179 deduction to $1 million worth of equipment eligible for the immediate write-off of expensing (although the amount is reduced if you place more than $2.5 million of new assets into service during any single year).

Be aware that if you claim depreciation for an automobile in a given tax year, you cannot switch back to claiming the standard mileage rate for the following tax year.

Education and Training

The cost of training classes, webinars, books, magazine subscriptions, research material, educational fees, travel, and other expenses related to business education and training are fully deductible.

The greatest part about education is that it grows your business even more if you attend the events you need to and listen to the proper tools. These could be industry specific. If you are in Direct Sales, the company you work with will usually have its own events. They could be personal development events such as those held by Les Brown, Tony Robbins, Eric Worre, or Grant Cardone. If you are attempting to grow your income, the events or tools are deductible.

If you are attempting to grow your income, the events or tools are deductible.

Fringe Benefits

I have dedicated an entire chapter to fringe benefits. These are benefits you offer your employees that are expenses for you but not included as income for them. This category is a win-win for both of you.

CHAPTER 6

How the New Tax Cuts and Jobs Act of 2017-2018 Will Affect Your Taxes

The new tax laws passed in December 2017 created lots of changes, and these changes are excellent for business owners, but not so much for individuals. The changes have also become a tremendous opportunity for small businesses to save a great deal of money in taxes. You must understand that tax rates and taxable income are equally important. Your taxable income will change if you are self-employed under the new tax laws. Even though most will profit, it is not automatic that everyone pays less taxes. You may need to change the way you run your business to get what you are entitled to.

Here are the new tax rates from 2017 to 2018:

TAX BRACKETS FOR SINGLE FILERS			
2017		2018	
10%	$0-$9,325	10%	$0-$9,525
15%	$9,326-$37,950	12%	$9,526-$38,700
25%	$37,951-$91,900	22%	$38,701-$82,500
28%	$91,901-$191,650	24%	$82,501-$157,500
33%	$191,651-$416,700	32%	$157,501-$200,000
35%	$416,701-$418,400	35%	$200,001-$500,000
39.60%	$418,401 or more	37%	$500,000 or more
Standard Deduction: $6,350		Standard Deduction: 12,000	
Personal Exemptions: $4,050		Personal Exemptions: none	

TAX BRACKETS FOR MARRIED FILERS			
2017		2018	
10%	$0-$18,650	10%	$0-$19,050
15%	$18,651-$75,900	12%	$19,051-$77,400
25%	$75,901-$153,100	22%	$77,401-$165,000
28%	$153,101-$233,350	24%	$165,001-$315,000
33%	$233,351-$416,700	32%	$315,001-$400,000
35%	$416,701-$470,700	35%	$400,001-$600,000
39.60%	$470,701 or more	37%	$600,001 or more
Standard Deduction: $12,600		Standard Deduction: $24,000	
Personal Exemptions: $8,100		Personal Exemptions: none	

Major Changes for Individuals

1. **The standard deduction** has essentially doubled, but personal exemptions have been eliminated—the standard deduction is $12,000 for single and $24,000 if you are married filing jointly.

Example: You are married and make $75,000 per year. You would subtract $24,000 from your income, leaving you with a taxable income of $51,000. Then you multiply your income by your tax bracket, leaving you with a tax savings of $2,673.

	OLD LAW	NEW LAW
Income	$75,000	$75,000
Standard deduction (married)	($12,700)	($24,000)
Taxable income	$62,300	$51,000
Taxes owed (using tax rates)	$8,412	$5,739

2. **Personal exemptions:** Although the standard deduction has increased, the personal exemption has been discontinued. The personal exemption was $4,100 per person who is a dependent. This includes kids still living in your home and your spouse.

3. **Increase in the Child Tax Credit:** To offset the personal exemption elimination, Congress increased the Child Care Credit. This has gone from the current $1,000 to $2,000 per qualifying child under age 17. Additionally, there is a $500 credit provided for certain non-child dependents. Also, up to $1,400 of this credit is refundable for each qualifying child. This was created to help people with lower incomes.

Example: If you have two children who are dependents, this is what the tax implication looks like.

	OLD LAW	NEW LAW
Income	$75,000	$75,000
Standard deduction (married)	($12,700)	($24,000)
Exemptions ($4,100/person)	($16,400)	$0
Taxable Income	$45,900	$51,000
Taxes Owed	$5,952	$5,739

However, the child credit makes a big difference; these are much better than deductions, as you are allowed savings dollar for dollar. (Note: the phase-out of this credit for single taxpayer earnings is at more than $200,000, and for married filing jointly at over $400,000.)

Example: This is what the Child Tax Credit looks like with two children.

	OLD LAW	NEW LAW
Income	$75,000	$75,000
Standard deduction (married)	($12,700)	($24,000)
Exemptions ($4,100/person)	($16,400)	$0
Taxable Income	$45,900	$51,000
Taxes Before Credits	$5,952	$5,739
Child Tax Credit	($2,000)	($4,000)
Taxes Owed	3,952	$1,739

4. **Property, state, and local taxes are capped at $10,000.** Before 2018, you could write off all of your property, state, and local taxes. All of these combined are now capped at $10,000. This may not affect as many people because of the increase in the standard deduction,

and less people will itemize.

Example: Scott pays $8,000 in state taxes, $28,000 in real estate taxes, and $2,000 in property taxes, totaling $38,000. This means that he will lose $28,000 in tax deductions and tens of thousands in taxes, as he does itemize, and even with the increase in the standard deduction will still itemize.

5. **Miscellaneous itemized deductions have been suspended until January 1, 2026.** This includes unreimbursed employee business expenses, tax preparation fees, safe deposit boxes, and non-business expenses. This also could include gambling losses; there is not a clear determination in this area yet.

6. **Casualty losses have been eliminated unless they occur in a federally declared disaster area.** Therefore, a person only receives a deduction when the government declares a particular area a disaster.

Example: If your home was infested with mold and you lost everything, because it is not considered a federal disaster, you do not get to claim the loss. Note: this makes it even more important to have great insurance coverage.

7. **Home equity line and home mortgage interest:** Homeowners can deduct the interest they pay on mortgage debt at up to $750,000 instead of $1 million under the old law. You can now deduct interest from a home equity line only if the money borrowed is used to repair or upgrade your home.

8. **Medical expense deduction threshold reduced:** Under the old tax law, you could only claim medical expenses if they exceeded 10 percent of your adjusted gross income. This was lowered to 7.5 percent under the new law, but only until January 1, 2019. This rule helps people if they have unusually high medical expenses.

Example: If someone makes $40,000 in income and has $10,000 in medical expenses, under this rule the patient can deduct anything that is greater than 7.5 percent of their income, which is $3,000, so anything above that number could be a deduction. If you have a high income, it is unlikely you'll be able to deduct your medical expenses—unless you own a business.

(Information from: IRC Section 213(f), as amended by Act Section 11027(a))

9. **Charitable contribution deduction limitation increased:** Under the old tax law, you were only able to get a deduction for cash contributions if the amount contributed was less than 50 percent of your income for public charities and between 20 and 30 percent for private charities. If you made $50,000, you can give away $25,000 to a public charity. In addition, any contributions of $250 or more needed an acknowledgment from the charity for proof of the donation. Under the new tax law, cash contributions made before January 1, 2026, can now be up to 60 percent of your adjusted gross income. This also applies to certain private foundations and contributions made on or after January 1, 2017. You no longer need to receive a receipt from the charity for contributions of $250 or more.

10. **Alimony deduction eliminated, and there is no income for the recipient.** Before the tax cuts law, you could deduct payments that qualified as alimony to your spouse; the spouse would then claim the income on their tax return. Under the new law, for any divorce or separation agreement executed after December 31, 2018—or executed before that date but modified after it—alimony is no longer deductible by the paying spouse. In addition, it cannot be claimed as income by the spouse who receives the money.

11. **The exclusion for moving expenses reimbursed by employer is suspended.** Beginning January 1, 2018, the exclusion for qualified moving expenses reimbursements is suspended—with the exception of members of the armed forces on active duty and for their spouses and dependents who move because of a military order. Under the old law, an employee could exclude qualified moving expenses reimbursements from his or her gross income and from his or her wages.

(IRC Section 132(g), as amended Section 11048)

12. **Repeal of the ACA (Affordable Care Act) individual mandate:** Under the old tax law, the Affordable Care Act required individuals who were not covered by a health plan to pay a penalty. This applied if they did not have minimum essential coverage. This has now been repealed. (The law is often more informally known as Obamacare.) At this time, the repeal is permanent.

(IRC Section 5000c, as amended by Act Section 11081)

13. **Expanded use of Section 529 funds for private school tuition:** Under the prior tax law, funds from a section 529 account could only be used for qualified higher education. This included college and graduate schools for tuition, fees, books, supplies, and required equipment as well as room and board if the student was enrolled at least half-time. This law was for eligible schools, including colleges and universities, vocational schools, and other post-secondary schools eligible to participate in a student aid program of the Department of Education for distributions made after December 31, 2017. The new law includes up to $10,000 of tuition at an elementary or secondary public, private, or religious school.

(IRC Section 529(7), as amended by Act Section 11032(a))

14. **Estate and gift changes:** Under the old tax law, the first $5 million was exempt from estate and gift taxes, adjusted for inflation. The new tax law doubled that amount to $10 million, also adjusted for inflation. It is expected that the exempt amount for 2018 will be $11.2 million. What does this mean for you? When your loved ones pass away, they can now gift $10 million plus inflation—tax free. This is a per-person amount, so a couple would be able to exempt approximately $22.4 million in 2018.

(IRC Section 2010c(3), as amended by Act Section 11061(a))

As you can see, most of the changes for individuals are not great and are actually taking away more than they

Let's take a look at the business changes—because there has never been a better time to own a business than today.

are giving. There will definitely be individuals paying more in the next year or so than in previous years. In later chapters, I will be sharing how you can get at least a percentage of the majority of these deductions back by something called redirecting expenses. By owning a business, you are able to claim most of these expenses as business deductions—or at least a percentage of them. Now let's take a look at the business changes—because there has never been a better time to own a business than today.

Major Changes for Businesses

1. **The pass-through entity deduction:** This is a new deduction that allows an additional 20 percent deduction for sole proprietorships, partnerships, and S corporations. This is huge for a business. *Example*: Your business makes $100,000 in net income. You only have to pay taxes on $80,000 because you receive $20,000 in a deduction due to the pass-through entity deduction.

2. **Vehicle depreciation changes:** Vehicle deductions are one of the biggest tax deductions you can have in a business, and there are two ways to take deductions. One way is the mileage method, and the other is the actual method. The easier and more conservative way is the mileage method. The government will allow you up to 84 1/2 cents deduction in 2018 for every mile you drive for

business purposes. Under the new tax laws, this is rarely going to be a great decision for you. *Example*: Your car averages 25 miles a gallon; you drive 25 miles. On one gallon, gas costs on average $2.50, so it costs you $2.50 to drive 25 miles. If you drive those 25 miles for business purposes, then the IRS will give you a deduction of $13.63—in other words, it lowers the amount of income you have to pay taxes on by $13.63. To determine how much money that will save you in taxes at the end of the year, you multiply that by your tax bracket. At an average tax bracket of 35 percent, including state and federal taxes, you save $4.77 in taxes. You can see, however, that using this throughout the year can save you thousands of dollars just by driving 10,000 miles for legitimate business purposes. You would save approximately $3,500.

Now for the actual method: this is calculated, just as it implies. At the end of the year you calculate the total cost for driving your car and multiply that by the percentage of miles you drive for business compared to the total mileage. *Example*: You had $15,000 in business expenses. You drive your vehicle 80 percent for business purposes; that would mean you have a deduction of $12,000 on your actual expenses. If you are in a 35 percent tax bracket, that would save you $4,200 in taxes. Also, with the actual cash method, you can find additional deductions for depreciation—and this is the area in which we see drastic changes this year. You can now depreciate your vehicles much quicker. Qualified trucks can be deducted 100 percent in the first year using the Section 179 deduction. (Note: it must meet all of the following criteria. It must not have any rear seating; it must be new to you; it must be on a truck chassis; it must have a six foot or greater cargo area; it must have a gross vehicle weight of 6,000 pounds or more.) Qualified vans and SUVs also can be depreciated 100 percent the first year. However, there is a rule that gives you temporary bonus depreciation for these vehicles; this rule phases out over time. Here are the requirements: it must be on a truck chassis, you must buy it in the same year you claim the depreciation, it must carry passengers, and it must have a gross vehicle weight of 6,000 pounds or more. Even if you don't buy one of the qualified vehicles that we just talked about, the new tax law will benefit you. You can depreciate cars much quicker now. Under the old tax law, with a $50,000 BMW 528—or any other luxury car—it would have taken eighteen years to depreciate if you drove it 100 percent for business. Under the new tax law, it will take about 5.8 years. You will start to see many business owners driving nicer cars. Below, I've placed a chart to see the difference in depreciation from 2017 to 2018. Not only can you claim depreciation, you also get to claim gas, oil changes, repairs, car washes, and more.

Please remember deductions are one of the most audited expenses, and you must keep a mileage log regardless of which method you use. Recording mileage can be tedious, but it is a requirement if you want to make sure you're keeping up and receiving all of your expenses.

YEAR	2017	2018
1	$11,160	$10,000
2	$5,100	$16,000
3	$3,050	$9,600
4	$1,875	$5,760

| 5 | $1,875 | $5,760 |
| 6 | $1,875 | $5,760 |

So what qualifies for business driving? Many people believe that their drive to and from work is tax deductible, but this is not true. Your commute to your main office is not tax deductible. However, if you run a business from your home, then all your business stops from your home are deductible. So, if you're going to the bank, you want to meet with a client, and you are going to pick up office supplies for your business, all are tax deductible if you have a regular job. In addition to your own business, then the direct commute to your job is not deductible regardless of whether you have a main office or a home office. Temporary business stops are stops that you don't make regularly or that you will not be visiting frequently for more than a year. Since you expect to go to the bank or the post office regularly for years to come, this is not a temporary business stop. However, visiting a client or prospect would be considered a temporary stop. *Example*: Going to the post office from your house is not tax deductible. However, if you leave your home to go to the post office and then go see a client, the deduction would include the mileage after the post office visit. If you make legitimate business stops outside your normal business area, then all round trip mileage is deductible as long as you will not be there more than a year. *Example*: You live in South Carolina and you attend a convention in Fort Lauderdale. That convention will be deductible since it is outside of your normal geographic area of business. If you were in Fort Lauderdale for a project that's expected to last more than a year, then the mileage would be deductible.

So, how do you turn your personal miles into business mileage? You must first understand how to mix business with pleasure. Let's say you want to drive and meet your parents for lunch. That is not a business trip. However, ask yourself: do I have a client I could stop and see on the way to my parents' house? If you do set up an appointment and do some business on the way there or the way back, then the mileage to and from the client becomes deductible. Therefore, the only portion of the trip not deductible is your lunch with your parents. And if you log this deduction, you have just saved some money.

3. **Meals and entertainment have changed drastically.** Eating out with a client can be a great way to grow your business. Did you know that many of your meals can be tax deductible? However, with the new tax law meals are still deductible—but entertainment is not. Please note: you can no longer take clients out to sporting events such as golf or to a football or baseball game. The new law still allows for a 50 percent reduction of your meals. If you follow the rules, you will be able to deduct many of the meals you eat out. If you take a client out and spend $75 on a dinner and follow the rules outlined below, you can deduct 50 percent, or $37.50, of the meal. If you're in the 35 percent tax bracket, this will save you $13.13 in taxes at the end of the year (35 percent times the $37.50 amount). A meal qualifies as a deduction if it meets the following criteria:

1) You must have the appointment set up in advance, and whoever you're eating with must expect to talk about business.

2) You must talk about business before, during, or after the meal at any place that is easy to talk about business. The information must be recorded soon after the meal. The following information is crucial to your deduction: who did you take out to eat; where did you eat; when did the expense occur; what did you talk about; what was the expense, such as a meal or drinks; and finally, how much did the meal cost? Most of this information can be found on your receipt, other than who you took out. The why is that it should be considered a business meal, so be certain that you add this to your receipt. Unfortunately, you are not able to deduct eating out with your spouse even if they are a business partner and you discuss business. There are a few exceptions: if you take out a client and they bring along their spouse or significant other, you can bring your spouse or significant other, and up to 50 percent of your spouse's meal is deductible. However, if your client does not bring along a spouse or significant other, then your spouse's meal is not deductible—unless both of you are working on the project together. *Example*: If both you and your spouse are mortgage brokers and will be helping out with the mortgage for your client's new home, then both of you are entitled to the 50 percent deduction.

4. **Business interest deductions** have now been decreased to 30 percent of your adjusted taxable income. This taxable income doesn't include:

- Non-business income, like gains from the sale of assets held for investment
- Business interest expense or business interest income
- Net operating loss deductions
- The new 20 percent qualified business income deduction
- Depreciation, amortization, or depletion

It may not be as attractive to finance your business anymore, because you may not get the tax deduction going forward, or it may be limited.

5. **Net operating loss (NOL) deduction.** In the past, if a business recorded a loss, it could take that loss back two years, or it could carry-forward the loss for twenty years. This has now changed. There are no prior-year NOL deductions, but you can carry forward the net operating loss deduction forever. Under the new tax law, the net operating loss can only be carried forward, and it is limited to 80 percent in any given year. An example of this would be a business that records a net operating loss of $50,000 in 2017. In 2018, however, that business ends up making $100,000. You can use the net operating loss to reduce your taxable income for 2018 by $40,000, which is 80 percent of $50,000. Whatever you did not use can be used in future years, so your business could apply that remaining $10,000 net operating loss in future years.

6. **The new C corporate tax rate:** The new corporate

tax rate is down 21 percent as opposed to previous corporate rates, which were 15, 25, 34, and 35 percent. This change is permanent, and the new rate is a flat tax, meaning it is the same for all C corporations.

7. **Equipment and property.** If your company uses a substantial amount of equipment and property, there is now a considerable increase in the dollar limits for equipment purchases. This is caused by changes made to the Section 179 tax code. Previous tax years offered a maximum deduction of $510,000, but now the maximum for 2018 for section 179 deduction is increased to $1 million, and there is a phaseout threshold amount increased to $2.5 million when it comes to property. The bonus depreciation amount is now 100 percent instead of 50 percent for the property purchased and placed in service after September 27, 2017. This is a huge deduction for a business. Section 179 has been expanded to include not only computers and machinery but also residential rental properties, roofs, HVAC units, fire alarms, and security devices.

8. **Lobbying activities.** Repeal of the deduction for local lobbying activities: the new tax law disallows the deduction for lobbying expenses with respect to legislation before local government bodies. This provision is effective for amounts paid or incurred on or after the date of enactment of the law.

9. **Credit for Family and Medical Leave.** Employer credit for paid family and medical leave: Internal Revenue

Code Section 45S provides a tax credit for employers who provide paid family and medical leave to their employees. Eligible employers may claim the credit, which is equal to a percentage of wages they pay to qualifying employees while they're on family and medical leave. The credit generally is effective for wages paid in taxable years of the employer beginning after December 31, 2017. The credit is a percentage of the amount of wages paid to a qualifying employee while on family and medical leave for up to twelve weeks per taxable year. The minimum percentage is 12.5 percent and is increased by 0.25 percent for each percentage point by which the amount paid to a qualifying employee exceeds 50 percent of the employee's wages, with a maximum of 25 percent. In certain cases, an additional limit may apply. A qualifying employee is any employee under the Fair Labor Standards Act who has been employed by the employer for one year or more and who, for the preceding year, had compensation of not more than a certain amount. For an employer claiming a credit for wages paid to an employee in 2018, the employee must not have earned more than $72,000 in 2017.

As you can see, the new tax law has drastically changed many things. We can also see that these changes are much better for the business owner as opposed to a salaried employee.

With these new tax law changes, it is imperative for you to have some sort of business on the side—even if you are a salaried employee. This will enable you to keep more of your money in your pocket.

CHAPTER 7

How to Hire Your Kids and Spouse and Lower Your Taxes

Kids are usually really expensive, but you can benefit from the expense of raising children by hiring your kids! If you own a business, there are things your children can do for you in your business. A few examples:

- Posting to social media
- Answering phones and emails to and from clients
- Sending mailers, products, or samples
- Filing paperwork
- Cleaning the office
- Helping with day-to-day transactions

You ask: How can I do this? Well, if you were to hire an employee or a subcontractor to do any of the above, the expenses would be deductible, right? So why not hire

your kids instead of someone else? Smart business owners realize children can be paid a reasonable wage if they
do legitimate work for your business. They in turn can
pay for what they want themselves, such as video games
or clothes. Not only is this good for you because of the
tax deductions, it teaches them how to manage their
own money. Also, kids do not have to have pay taxes on
the first $12,000 of income because of the new standard
deduction. This is a true win-win for everyone.

Note that if you are treating your business like a sole
proprietorship or partnership and your kids are under
18, there is no social security or unemployment taxes to
deduct or match, and taxes do not have to be withheld
if they are under the $12,000 income mark. If you have
an S Corp, you do have to withhold FICA taxes. There
are ways around this as well, however. This is huge for
you and your business. So hire your kids now instead of
paying their bills!

I have six kids. If I paid them $12,000 per year (I am
already spending it on them!), that would be $72,000 in
deductions for my business, and they would not have to
pay taxes.

Example: You pay your child $12,000 in wages for 2018
in your self-employed business. You are able to deduct
wages of $12,000 on your Schedule C or Schedule E if
it relates to rental property, assuming that those wages
are reasonable. You would then pay no social security
or unemployment taxes. Your child would report the
$12,000 as income but then deduct the $12,000 standard
deduction. If you are in a 39.6 percent tax bracket, this
would produce a tax savings for you of $4,752 from fed-

eral taxes alone. If you paid your child more than $12,000 in wages, you would save 29.6 percent (39.6 percent minus the 10 percent bracket for children).

Your child could also put away $5,500 a year of the earnings into a Roth IRA that would allow the interest and appreciation of the IRA to be tax-free to the child if used for college.

Now, I have clients who ask, all the time, "At what age can I hire my kids?" There is a tax court case that held that you could hire a child who is at least seven years old. If they are younger than seven, if you use social media and print advertising, hiring your child as a model may work. This has not been precedented yet, but if you are willing to pay for stock photos and models, who says that you can't pay your kids instead? No one, yet!

The one thing that you must make sure of with your children is that you are paying them a reasonable salary and that you have a record of what they are doing for you in your business.

The one thing that you must make sure of with your children is that you are paying them a reasonable salary and that you have a record of what they are doing for you in your business. What is reasonable? What are you willing to pay someone else to do the same job? If you would hire a bookkeeper for $15 an hour, you can hire your child to do the same for $13 an hour. This should be considered reasonable.

Documentation is key when hiring relatives. There

needs to be either a written or electronic time sheet that states:

- Date worked
- Tasks performed
- Hours worked

The most important part is that you actually have to pay them! The money must go into an account, or you must be able to prove that they received payment. Make sure that you also have filled out the proper paperwork for employment including a W-4, I-9, and that you have an employment application and contract.

So, go hire your kids and stop paying for their stuff—things like college, books, video games, and all the other things that kids want. Even "big kids"—those older than eighteen—qualify for this. You just have to pay the Social Security taxes, and so do they.

Now let's talk about your spouse. When you hire your spouse, you must take out social security, so the key here is to pay them minimum wage and give them as many fringe benefits as possible. The main purpose of hiring your spouse is allowing the business to write off medical expenses that would not be deductible because of the threshold amount being 7.5 percent of your adjusted gross income (AGI). Self-employed people are not allowed to be covered under this plan, but that can be bypassed by hiring a spouse or forming a corporation and creating a self-insured medical plan that is in addition to medical insurance. This would cover copays, deductibles, coinsurance, dental, braces, medical miles, chiropractic, and more. The IRS allows that one employee is OK for a medical reimbursement account. You can reimburse your spouse for all medical expenses and it would be considered a fringe benefit to him or her, so it would not be taxable for the spouse, and the business gets the deduction. The great part is that you get to maintain full control over the plan and can make it as broad or as narrow as you want.

The steps required to set up a self-insured medical reimbursement plan:

- If not, form a regular corporation and have the corporation approve the plan at a board of directors meeting.

- Have the medical reimbursement plan drafted.

- Make your spouse the primary insured on the plan and elect for family coverage.

- Pay the medical bills directly or reimburse any family member for any medical expense incurred.

- The plan needs to stay in existence for at least three years.

- Meet with your accountant annually to have a per-year employee maximum payout to assure that the total salary and payout are reasonable for the hours and work performed.

- Remember, you can only utilize these deductions after the plan has been implemented.

Also, you must make sure that you do not discriminate in favor of the owners, so if you have other employees, you must cover all full-time employees, meaning the plan must cover 70 percent or more of all employees. There are exceptions to this rule, including part-time workers, employees under twenty-five years of age, employees with less than three years of service, and nonresident aliens.

CHAPTER 8

Getting Money Out of Your Company Tax Free

This chapter will not only help you save more money in taxes, it will also help your employees save more money in taxes. The category of *fringe benefits* is one of the greatest secrets for business owners. Most small businesses don't even know what fringe benefits are. Fringe benefits is the umbrella term for any benefits, from health insurance to paying for weekly team lunches, that an employer provides to an employee, contractor, board member, or business partner. Many fringe benefits are considered tax-free by the IRS and can be a great value-add for your employees. If starting a successful small business is the engine behind riches, then fringe benefits are the wheels and the frame around the engine, Sandy Botkin wrote in the book *Lower Your Taxes—Big Time*.[2]

In this chapter, I'm going to share with you what's required to establish each benefit and also what to do to audit-proof each benefit. Some benefits can be offered to both owners and employees while others have limitations on what can be offered to owners or stockholders. Although these benefits assume you're operating as a corporation, many apply to other entities such as sole proprietors and LLCs.

The following is taken from IRS 15B (2018).

Cafeteria Plans

A cafeteria plan, including an Flexible Spending Account, provides participants an opportunity to receive qualified benefits on a pretax basis. It is a written plan that allows your employees to choose between receiving cash or taxable benefits instead of certain qualified benefits for which the law provides an exclusion from wages. If an employee chooses to receive a qualified benefit under the plan, the fact that the employee could have received cash or a taxable benefit instead won't make the qualified benefit taxable. Generally, a cafeteria plan doesn't include any plan that offers a benefit that defers pay. Also, certain life insurance plans maintained by educational institutions can be offered as a benefit even though they defer pay.

Qualified benefits. A cafeteria plan can include the following benefits:

- Disability insurance

- Long-term care insurance

- Medical insurance

- Group term life insurance

- Adoption assistance
- Qualified pension or profit-sharing plan
- Dependent care assistance. Group term life insurance coverage (including costs that can't be excluded from wages)
- Health savings accounts (HSAs). Distributions from an HSA may be used to pay eligible long-term care insurance premiums or qualified long-term care services.
- Credits for additional paid vacation weeks

Cafeteria plans are nearly the ideal benefit. Setting up one benefit can offer your employees many benefits, as discussed above in the IRS section, thus saving lots of time, legal and accounting fees, and money on multiple benefits. The only problem is that Congress limits cafeteria plans from helping most owners and officers of a business. Cafeteria plans are usually not implemented in small businesses because the plan is not available for owners. This fringe benefit is a no-brainer for small businesses if you have any employees.

Bulletproofing the Benefit

The benefits generally must be provided to all employees on a nondiscriminatory basis, although you can have a waiting period for eligibility of up to three years. Also, you must make sure the cafeteria plan is in writing and contains specific information about the plan. You can't just keep the plan quiet and hope your employees choose nothing. The plan cannot discriminate on the benefits provided. Also, more than 25 percent of the total of the non-tax benefit cannot go to key employees. The key employees are a group that comprises highly compensated employees who are generally making more than $120,000 per year, officers, individuals who own more than 5 percent of the stock, and spouses independent of anyone noted above. You must also cover everyone who has been with the company for more than three years. The participants must make a specific collection of the benefits they are choosing and make this election at the beginning of the year or when they start work, whichever comes first.

Here are more of my personal thoughts on this option: the cafeteria plan is an amazing benefit for your employees even if you do not get to take it as a business owner. There are some cases that will allow you to use this if the corporation does not discriminate and it does not provide more than 25 percent of the benefits to the owners or certain key or highly compensated employees.

(Section 125(d) and 125 (g)(3) of the IRC)

Tax-Free Use of Property, Equipment, and Services

This is one of the broadest ways to obtain tax-free fringe benefits. This benefit is also known as working-condition fringe benefits. These types of benefits are defined as "any property or services given to an employee by an employer that would have been deductible or depreciable by the employee as a business expense had the employee paid for the property or services." This only applies to employees and not their dependents. Here are some examples: memberships in business-oriented associations, membership-based websites for businesses, cell phones, computers, business-related books, business publications, business events, and more.

Example: Sally owns an accounting firm. She wants a membership to BNI, which is a business networking group. She also wants to attend numerous business-related seminars and receive sales publications to better her business. Her corporation may provide Sally with the membership, publications, and seminars as tax-free working-condition fringe benefits because Sally could have deducted the cost update had she spent the money herself. Why is it important that Sally receives the working-condition fringe benefit? As of 2018, there is no longer a way for Sally to deduct these benefits from her personal tax return because unreimbursed employee business expenses are no longer deductible. This benefit can be provided only to the officers or directors or other highly compensated employees of the company.

Example: Your corporation offers cell phones and computers to highly compensated employees and owners. These benefits are fully deductible by your corporation and tax free to the employees even though they are not provided to all employees. In addition, independent contractors are allowed to be given working condition fringe benefits on a tax-free basis as long as they don't involve parking or product testing. Self-employed owners are not deemed employees under this rule, but they can deduct these items as business deductions without any limitations; thus, in effect, they get the benefits too.

(Section 132(d) of the IRC. Letter Ruling 19992903.

Section 1.131-5q of the ITR. Section 1.132-1(b) of the ITR)

Recap: *This is available to all business entities. You can fully discriminate with this deduction for owners and highly compensated employees, meaning you can decide who to give this benefit to.*

Tax-Free Day Care Assistance

You can provide day care tax free to all employees up to a maximum of $5,000 per year or $2,500 if married filing separately; the self-employed are considered employees under this rule as well. Even partnerships can offer this benefit to partners who are treated as employees. You can opt to pay the employees' day care directly or reimburse employees for the expenses. However, you cannot discriminate in favor of highly compensated people, owners, or stockholders who have a 5 percent or greater interest in stock or profits of the company, and there are limitations on the benefits that can accrue to the owners as well.

In order to receive the benefits tax free you must meet the following requirements.

Dependents must be under the age of thirteen, or either physically or mentally incapable of caring for themselves if over thirteen. You must have a separate written plan and you must notify all employees of the availability of the benefit. You cannot discriminate in favor of highly compensated employees, owners who hold more than 5 percent of the company, or stockholders of greater than 5 percent. The employees must provide documentation to the employer such as the name, address, and social security number or tax ID number of the provider. Also, even if you give this benefit to everyone, you can't have more than

25 percent of the total benefits go to any stockholder or business owner who owns more more than 5 percent of the stock of the business.

(IRC Section 129(a)(1), 129(a)(2), 129(b)(1), 129(e)(3), 129(e)(4))

Note: For those taking care of parents and children at the same time, a great way to get your parents some money tax free is if your parents take care of your children. This accomplishes two things at once.

There are so many more fringe benefits available out there, some better than others. I would advise you to learn as much as you can about fringe benefits, as they are truly the answer to get money tax free out of your corporation or company and also help your employees at the same time.

Recap: *This is available to all business entities. Discrimination is not allowable. And there is a limitation that no more than 25 percent of the benefits can go to 5 percent or more of the stockholders or owners.*

(Section 129(a)(2), 129(a)(1), 129(b)(1), 129(e)(3))

No Additional Cost Fringe Benefits

A company can provide services to employees on a tax-free basis if it meets these conditions: the services are offered to customers in the ordinary course of business and the company doesn't incur substantial additional cost in providing these benefits.

Example: ABC accounting firm provides tax preparation for its employees at no additional cost. This benefit is no increased cost to the company; therefore, it would be a tax-free benefit to the employee.

(Section 132(j)(1))

Recap: *This is available to all types of business entities. No discrimination is allowed and there are no limits to benefits offered to owners or highly compensated employees.*

Employer Education Assistance

Generally, any educational expense paid for an employee or a member of an employee's family is deductible by the company but taxable to the employee unless you have one of the exceptions below. You can set up an educational assistance program for your employees and pay up to $5,250 per year for tuition, fees, books, and supplies; however, you cannot provide meals, lodging, transportation, or payments for sports games or hobbies unless they are part of a degree program. No discrimination is allowed in favor of business owners or highly compensated employees; however, employees of sole proprietorships can use this benefit. The problem is that no more than 5 percent of the total benefits can be paid to a stockholder who owns more than 5 percent of the stock or to an individual who owns 5 percent or more of the business, even if you don't discriminate in any way. Therefore, if you have very few employees, this benefit will not work for you or your immediate family but will work for your employees.

Recap: *This benefit is available to all entities. Discrimination is not allowable. No more than 5 percent of benefits can go to 5 percent-or-more stockholders or owners. There is a limitation of $5,250 per employee per year.*

(Section 127(a)(1) and 127(c) of the IRC. Section

1.132-1(f) of the ITR and Section 1.132-5(d)(2) of the ITR)

Gym and Athletic Facilities

You are allowed to deduct the cost of exercise equipment, tennis courts, swimming pools, and golf courses and provide these items tax free to your employees and, if you're incorporated, to yourself. In order to make this benefit tax free you must meet several tests: The equipment or gym must be operated by the company; the equipment must be used substantially by employees of the company, their spouses, and their dependent children; and the equipment or gym generally must be on the company premises or at least owned by the employer.

There are couple of important things to realize with this benefit. You cannot provide your employees with a gym membership as it would not substantially be used by your employees. Also, the facility must be run by the company, which means you cannot use a resort with a facility, such as a tennis court or swimming pool. However, you can also allow partners and employees who are separated from the company either through disability or retirement. Under this benefit you can deduct and provide, on a tax-free basis, the following types of items: exercise equipment, gyms, tennis courts, swimming pools, and golf courses. Because self-employed individuals are not considered to be employees, they ordinarily cannot give themselves this fringe benefit. However, if you are employed and you hire your spouse to work for your company, or other family members, they become your employees. If you place a gym or a swimming pool in the location where your family employees work, you may be able to deduct the cost of the gym or swimming pool. It is vital that employees or their family members use the facility. It is best to keep a log for everyone using the facility. You can also pay rent to another company that's operating a facility for its own employees and be entitled to this fringe benefit.

Recap: *This benefit is available to all business entities. Discrimination (defined here, narrowly, as making choices about who and who cannot use the benefit, based on employee status) is allowable for this benefit.*

(Section 1.132-1€(4) of the ITR and Letter Ruling 9029026)

Company-Provided Vehicles

When a corporation provides a company vehicle, the employees are taxed on the personal use of the vehicle. Once company cars are provided, it is crucial to keeping a good mileage log because this documents how much of the car was used for business purposes and how much was used for personal purposes, which is the portion that is taxable. There are three different ways or methods to determine the amount of taxable income. The first method is the annual lease value method, and this is definitely not the best way to go but may be the only one available to utilize because of the limitation of the other methods. The cents-per-mile method can only be used if the vehicle is inexpensive. The commuting value method is the best and cheapest method for tax treatment on a company car. This is very limited for owners and officers.

Recap: *This benefit is available to all business entities. Discrimination is allowable for this benefit. And there are no limitations on benefits to owners or highly compensated employees.*

(Section 1.61-21 of the ITR)

Company-Provided Trips for Employees and Spouses

Many companies provide their top employees, especially salespeople, with conventions at various locations around the world, not only to reward them but also to allow them more education. This also gives the employees incentives to work harder and make more money for the company. For the trip to be tax deductible, there must be training or continuing education activities that are the primary focus for the biggest part of the day. This does not include weekend days that are sandwiched between business days. The employee must attend four hours and one second of meetings each day for it to be considered a business day. Travel days are included as well, and these do not require meetings.

The big question is what happens if the spouse comes along. The key point is this: the spouse cannot be there just to keep you company.

The big question is what happens if the spouse comes along. You can bring the spouse and it is tax-free if your spouse is licensed in the field you are licensed in or if your spouse can make money for you or the company at the event. The key point is this: the spouse cannot be there just to keep you company. If the spouse is an employee of the taxpayer, this would also be tax free. If the spouse is helping at the event, such as checking people in or attending courses related to their duties, then their attendance is tax free.

Recap: *This benefit is available to all business entities. Discrimination is allowable with this benefit. And there are no limitations on benefits to owners or highly compensated employees. You must understand that for tax free reimbursement for spouses, that spouse must be licensed in business, work for the company, or provide convention duties.*

(Section 1.132-5(t)(1) of the ITR)

Tax-Free Lodging and Meals

Under limited conditions, a company can provide tax-free housing to its employees if they meet the following conditions: the lodging is for the convenience of the employer; the lodging and/or food is provided on the business premises of the company; the lodging must be accepted by the employee as a condition of employment.

Example: The owner of a storage facility that is open 24/7 could supply tax-free lodging because the employee must be able to handle emergencies, manage the facility, and provide a watchful eye on the facility.

In order to provide tax-free lodging and meals, the employer must pay for the employee and provide them directly, and the employee cannot be reimbursed for meals or lodging they pay for themselves.

There are some exclusions for meals. Meals must be

provided for the benefit of the employer and furnished for noncompensatory business reasons. There are numerous ways to use this benefit, including a short business meal during working hours. If the lunch is typically under forty-five minutes, the meal can be provided. If you need your employees to work through lunch or have a short lunch break, you can provide them with meals on a tax-free basis.

If an employee is provided tax-free lodging they are also entitled to tax free meals because they are required to live on the company premises as a condition of the job.

Meals that are provided to restaurant employees are tax-free whether furnished before, during, or after their shift. More restaurants should use this benefit to retain and attract employees.

Meals can be provided tax free as well if the employees are available for emergency calls during their lunch break.

Meals can be provided tax free if there are insufficient eating facilities near the workplace. Here is a great example: I have a client who buys groceries for all of the employees, provides a kitchen, and someone cooks every day. The reason for this plan: there are not ample eating facilities nearby, and the employees are needed to work during lunch.

Meals that are provided to restaurant employees are tax-free whether furnished before, during, or after their shift. More restaurants should use this benefit to retain and attract employees.

Meals furnished to more than 50 percent of all employees are always tax free.

Example: A law firm provides meals to their paralegals when they are working on a case, in court, or on depositions. They provide meals for three of the five employees; therefore, the meal is tax free. Also, if you provide a meal for a lunch meeting, and provide it for 50 percent or more of the employees, it is tax free.

Meals provided at lunch conferences are deductible, even if off premises, and can be used even if only for senior officers of the company. For good business reasons, meals can be furnished to officers and directors on a discriminatory basis. There is an interesting exception for meals that I learned through Sandy Botkins's book *Lower Your Taxes—Big Time.* There was an interesting case that may provide a lot of small business owners with tax-free meals and company-provided housing. It involved a husband and wife who were the sole owners of a large farm, which was leased to a corporation owned by the children of the owner, whose last name was McDowell. That's the only business that the McDowell Corporation had: to lease out the land. The tenant, the children's corporation, was engaged in ranching operations and was required to keep the buildings and other improvements in good condition. McDowell retained the right to inspect the property. McDowell actually lived on the land through most of the year and made daily inspections of the leased land. The tax court held that the meals and lodging furnished by the corporation to the McDowells were tax free.[3] What does this mean to you? This case has many applications, and here's an example: Sally owns an accounting firm using a corporation. She's required to work out of her home and runs her accounting firm out of her home on a daily basis. She receives calls from clients in her home and her employees work from home. She meets with her clients at least weekly and all of her files and office materials are in her home. It would appear that, based on the McDowell case, she may be able to receive corporate meals and lodging tax free. This has not been tested in court; please understand that if you use it, there is no case law to fall back on yet, but it seems logical. Understand that this will not work for sole proprietors; it would only work for home-based business owners who are incorporated.

Tax-free lodging recap: *This benefit is available to all business entities except for sole proprietors. Discrimination is allowable for this benefit, and there are no limitations on benefits to owners or highly compensated employees.*

Tax-free meals recap: *This benefit is available to all business entities except owners of sole proprietorships. Discrimination is not allowable, but there are some exceptions for restaurant employees, emergency work, and lunch conferences. There are no limitations on benefits to owners or highly compensated employees.*

(Section 1.119-1 of the ITR, 119(b) of the ITC)

De Minimis Fringe Benefits and Occasional Supper Money

De minimis is Latin for "minimal," so these are benefits of a minimal nature. Your company can provide these to any employee even if it discriminates in favor of officers or highly compensated people, property, or services, under both of the following conditions: the value of the property or services is so small or inconsequential as to not warrant an accounting of it; and if the property or services are not provided too frequently. Even if a fringe benefit were smaller but one you provided daily, it would not be deemed *de minimis.* Please note, again: it must be infrequent and inconsequential to be a de minimis fringe benefit. Examples include weekly coffee or donuts, holiday gifts of low value, holiday turkeys if less than $25, free soft drinks, and occasional theater and season tickets.

Recap: *This benefit is available to all business entities except owners of sole proprietorships. Discrimination is allowable in this benefit, and there are no limits on benefits for owners or highly compensated employees.*

(Section 1.132-6 of the ITR. Section 132€1) of the IRS)

Qualified Pension and Profit Sharing

There are two extremely important reasons to offer qualified pension and profit sharing. One of those allows a large deduction, but the other is the legal protection against lawsuits, provided from qualified plans. The most popular and recommended plans among small businesses today are the profit-sharing plan, SEP (or Simplified Employee Pension) plan, defined benefit plan, and Simple IRAs. The profit-sharing plan allows you to put away in any business for any employee up to 25 percent of his or her wages. If you're self-employed, up to 25 percent of the net income with the company can be contributed. That's a maximum contribution of $54,000 for 2018 per employee. This plan is very flexible; the amount of the employee's wages that you can contribute every year can vary. So, if one year you want to contribute 10 percent and in the next year you want to contribute 25 percent, you can do so. There are some drawbacks. Discrimination is not allowed to owners or highly compensated employees. You must cover all full-time employees that have been with the company three years or longer. This plan is extensive to set up and requires filing expensive forms with the IRS.

Simplified Employee Pension plans allow you to contribute up to 25 percent of your net income if you're self-employed, or 25 percent of an employee's wages. This plan has a maximum contribution limit of $54,000 for 2018. A company can vary its contributions from year to year. Just like the profit sharing plan, SEPs are inexpensive to set up. Also, there are no complex annual filings, so administrative fees and expenses are low. SEP plans are nondiscriminatory. Sole proprietors also can use SEP plans, and they work great if you have few or no employees.

Defined Benefit Plan

This plan is very different and uses an actuary to compute how much you and your employees may contribute in order to get a set retirement income. A defined benefit plan normally allows you to contribute much more than other plans, especially if the workers are over fifty years of age. You would figure how much you need at retirement and work backward to determine the amount you must contribute. Since the older the worker—the less time there is to build up their retirement income—older workers can contribute much more than younger ones. The maximum yearly contribution to the fund benefit plan is a whopping $55,000 per year in 2018. There are two major drawbacks to this plan: the first is it is the most administratively expensive plan available. Second, there's very little flexibility to this plan. You have to contribute a set amount each year regardless of profitability of the company.

Simple IRAs

Simple IRAs are like traditional IRAs, except that with an IRA you can contribute up to 100 percent of your wages, with a maximum contribution of $12,500 in 2018. If you're over 50, you get to contribute an extra $3,000 in catch-up contribution. What is so different with a Simple IRA is that the employee, and not employer, makes most of the contributions. The employer need only match employee contribution if the employee makes a contribution for the year. A simple IRA allows an employee to contribute up to $12,500 in 2018. The employer only needs to match up to 3 percent of their wages. Although a SEP allows for much greater contribution, if you have several employees, I recommend setting up a simple IRA. The overall contribution by the owner may be less than with the SEP, but the benefit of not contributing as much for employees may greatly offset this. If a company wants to contribute as much as possible on behalf of its employees, a SEP may be a better choice.

Recap: *This benefit is available to all business entities. Discrimination is not allowable, but there are some exceptions such as a three-year waiting period. There are no limits to certain people, but there is an overall contribution limit.*

(Sections 404(a)(3)(a), 404(a)(8)(D) and 415(c)(1) of the IRC)

CHAPTER 9

How to Structure Your Business for the Greatest Tax Savings

When first starting a business, people tend to operate as cheaply as possible. Because of this, they may start operating the business in their personal name and not a business name. Some may go as far as getting an LLC but still claim their income through their personal tax return. But most do not take that a step further and operate their LLC as an S Corporation for tax purposes. Most business owners are not doing the proper requirements that are required for an S Corp election and could jeopardize their election status.

In this chapter, you will see all the entity types as well as the advantages and disadvantages for each. I am going to share with you what I feel the best entity is for the majority of businesses, especially small to medium-sized ones. Also, with the new tax laws that include the pass-through entity deduction, this decreaes your taxable business income by 20 percent. But in order to keep your S Corporation status, there are some things that you must do—and this chapter will teach you those.

SOLE PROPRIETORSHIP

This is by far the most popular entity, but that does not mean you should be one. Most people get started this way because it is cheap and easy, and if you do not create an entity, this is not really an entity, but this allows you to operate in business, and the income and expenses from the business are then claimed on your personal tax return on Schedule C.

The Benefits

A sole proprietorship is easy and simple to form. This entity occurs by default if you do not actively form another type of entity with the state. You are in setup mode once you start incurring expenses, and you are officially in business when you make your first sale. There may be business license requirements in your city or county, but there are no required filings for a city, county, or state return. You would use your social security number, and you are not even required to have a tax ID number unless you are going to have sales tax or payroll filings.

The Downside

There are three major issues when it comes to being a sole proprietorship: 1) exposure to liability; 2) self-employment tax; and 3) audit risk.

I am not an attorney, nor do I claim to be one, but

most everyone knows that if you are a sole proprietor, your personal assets are completely exposed when operating your business.

The second downside is the self-employment taxes for sole proprietors are 15.3 percent on their net income under $100,000 and 2.9 percent on anything above that. This is a huge amount of money that most sole proprietors do not even realize they owe. It is extremely important for sole proprietors to maximize their expenses so they can keep their income down as much as possible. It is also extremely important to monitor your income if you are a sole proprietor to make sure that you convert to an S Corporation, or create an LLC and treat it as an S Corp for tax purposes, saving you tens of thousands of dollars.

$100,000 Revenue
– $25,000 Expenses
= $75,000 Net Income. At 15.3 percent self-employment tax = $11,475

This is on top of state and federal taxes! Along with the liability, you can see that being a sole proprietor can really cost you more than you could ever pay to set up your business as an LLC or S Corp if you are generating an income.

The third problem is that sole proprietors are the most likely to be audited by the IRS. If you are going to be more aggressive with your tax write-offs, you do not need to be operating as a sole proprietorship.

When Does It Work?

The first instance in which a sole proprietorship works is when you are just getting started with a business idea and you are not sure where it is headed. If you are not operating fully, it can be too much to set up a formal company at the start. However, once liability becomes a concern and you are committed to what you are doing, you need to consult with an accountant and attorney to consider which entity is best for you and your situation.

The second is when you are hiring your children who are under eighteen. This would be extremely helpful in saving additional taxes. This type of company is called a *family support company*, and it charges your formal business entities to provide support and management services. Then, you do not have to deduct FICA taxes of 7.65 percent from your kids, and you do not have to pay the matching 7.65 percent FICA taxes.

Example: You have three kids under eighteen and pay them $12,000 per year in income. This would save your children $918 each in FICA taxes and save the company $2,754 in matching FICA taxes.

Understand that there may be other licenses that are needed. You may need a business license for your state, city, or county. If you have payroll, you will also have to obtain a federal and state ID number as well as an unemployment tax ID number. You will want to consult an accountant or attorney to make sure this is all set up properly. Also, I suggest you not go with an incorporation service. There are many questions that need to be answered and instructions that you should receive with the formation of your first company.

PARTNERSHIPS

The Benefits

The same benefits apply to partnerships as do sole proprietorships. They are easy and simple to form. You will need a federal ID number as there is a separate partnership return that will need to be filed.

The Downside

Talk about liability: the worst part of having a partnership is the liability that you are personally responsible for—not only for your actions but the actions of your partner. It is bad enough to be liable for what you do and can control, but to be liable for someone else is an entirely different ball game. *Example*: If your partner goes to the bank and borrows $25,000 in the name of the business, you are liable to pay that back if the partner does not. Also, taxes for the business are 100 percent owed by both parties until one party or both pay their share.

You also have the same exposure to self-employment taxes as the sole proprietor. Make sure if

Talk about liability: the worst part of having a partnership is the liability that you are personally responsible for—not only for your actions but the actions of your partner.

you choose this route that you have a proper operating agreement in place. I have seen one too many clients who went into business with friends and family and did not have an operating agreement and ended up in tax debt, personal debt, and/or did not receive their share of what was owed to them.

C-CORPORATION

The Benefits

There are two main benefits to being a C-Corporation. They are asset protection and the corporate veil. Assuming that the owners and officers of the corporation act with due care and within the scope of their responsibilities and duties, they are personally protected from the operations of the company.

The second benefit is raising capital since you have the ability to sell stock. So if you plan to need lots of capital, then this entity may be right for you.

The Downside

The biggest downfall for a C-Corporation is the double taxation on corporate profits. The C-Corporation pays taxes on the net income (highest rate is 21 percent due to new tax law changes) and then the individual owners pay taxes on the dividends they take out of the company.

The cost of setting up a C-Corporation is also a drawback.

When Does It Work?

If you plan to have one hundred or more shareholders, you are required to have a C-Corporation. Also, if you plan to go public, this choice is a must.

Also, some accountants will tell you there are more deductions that exist in a C-Corporation, but I disagree with this. Because of the double taxation, I have not seen where it is beneficial for any of my clients to be a C-Corporation. Speak to your accountant or attorney about this before you make the decision.

S-CORPORATION

The Benefits

This is by far my favorite entity: the S-Corporation. One of the greatest things about this entity is that the IRS allows you to be an LLC but to be treated as an S-Corporation for tax purposes. Most of my clients are an LLC treated as an S Corp. However, I have others that are true S-Corporations. There are many benefits.

What is a reasonable salary? What would you be willing to pay someone to replace you?

The number one benefit is to allow you to save on self-employment taxes. Those with an S-Corporation are required to take a reasonable salary, and the remainder is just included in their bottom line. What is a reasonable salary? What would you be willing to pay someone to replace you? I usually find that

30 percent of your net income is a good number to pay payroll on, but when you have a low income, you should claim a higher rate.

Example: If your net income is $36,000 and you work full-time in your business, you may want to claim $15,000. If you are making $75,000 in net income, I would suggest $25,000. Make sure you speak with your tax strategist to ensure you are claiming what you should.

There is no corporate tax or self-employment tax on the net income of an S-Corporation. Through a K-1, which is part of the 1120S, it flows through to the personal tax return and taxes are paid on your Form 1040.

$100,000 Revenue
– $25,000 Salary at 15.3 percent self-employment tax
– 25,000 Expenses
= $50,000 Net Income

With this example, $50,000 would flow through your personal tax return without paying self-employment taxes of 15.3%. The tax savings are $7,650. This is *huge* for a small business. And that money could be used to grow the company, for retirement, or could help put your kids through college.

The second reason is asset protection. Just like a C-Corporation, if the owners and operators act within their responsibilities and the duties of the company, there is no personal liability from the business operations.

The Downside
There are not a lot of downsides for an S-Corporation,

but it does require more paperwork. You must pay yourself a paycheck. You also must pay payroll taxes and file payroll tax returns quarterly. Also, payroll taxes must be paid.

The cost to set up an S-Corporation is higher than a Sole Proprietorship or LLC, but the benefits definitely outweigh the price.

The last is that this is not a great entity to hold property in and later sell at an appreciated value. Also, if you have partners, it is tough to distribute partnership profits to help with tax planning. There are better ways to set this up. Speak with a tax strategist on your individual situation.

When Does It Work?

When you need this for asset protection, you have a strong reason to set up an S-Corporation. The second main reason is when you start making a net income in your business and the self-employment tax savings are higher than the cost of being set up as an S-Corporation. I tend to find that it is feasible at about $25,000 in net income.

LLC

The Benefits

An LLC is used mainly to store assets. They limit your personal liability to the business.

Second, there is an option to set up an LLC and treat it as an S-Corporation for tax purposes. This is the greatest thing for my clients as LLCs are not expensive to get started and the S-Corp election allows for massive self-employment tax savings as discussed earlier.

Third, profit and losses for partners can be handled easier through this structure than through an S-Corp, as this type of entity is treated as a Partnership if there are partners. But partners are not liable for each other's actions if you use an LLC for the partnership.

When Does It Make Sense?

First, it makes sense if you have any property, including rental, investment, or commercial.

Second, it makes sense when you go into partnership with someone to limit the liability.

Please take time to get a tax consultation before setting up your business, as setup is crucial. LLCs are great as they are easy to set up—but not so easy to unwind.

Summary: In my opinion, after eighteen years of experience, I find that the greatest flexibility with the best savings is an LLC and to treat that as an S-Corporation for tax purposes by requesting the S Corp Election. This allows my clients to get the self-employment tax savings and does not cost them as much as an S-Corporation. Their liability is also limited, making this a great entity type.

Their liability is also limited, making this a great entity type.

CHAPTER 10

Why You Must Add a Home-Based Business If You Don't Already Have One
(Even if you already have a traditional business)

How far in debt are you? Did you ever ask yourself where all the money went from your paycheck? Let me tell you three things that every American needs to know.

- #1 - Did you know the average American household makes $61,000 per year?

- #2 - Did you know that same household will pay an average of $12,000 per year in taxes (FICA, Federal, State, Local)? This leaves the household $49,000 per year.

- #3 - Did you know the Average Cost of Living in

America is $53,000, leaving the household with a $4,000 deficit or debt.

- #4 - Did you know that by having a home-based business the average household can save $4,000 to $8,000 per year in taxes if you just attempt to earn an income?

Let's do the math on these statistics. When you combine the average income, the average tax rate, and factor in the average cost of living, the sad fact is that the average household is heading deeper in debt and is getting worse off financially every single year; hence the reason why people are so far into credit card debt and student loan debt.

How do these statistics affect you? Maybe you make more than the average or maybe less, but whatever your income, I'm sure you'd like to find a way to keep more of the money you make. All of us have to find a way to offset income/cost of living disparity to avoid creating annual debt. There are only two ways this can be done. You can either 1) increase your income; or 2) decrease taxes.

Here's my point. Don't choose between them; do *both* by starting your own home-based business. Changing your tax status will change your life and your bank account.

Most people will try to solve the income issue and pick up a second job, thinking they are going to get ahead by increasing their income. However, as they increase their income, their taxes go up as well, even their tax bracket, which brings a whole new set of considerations, such as:

- increased taxes on all earned money

- decrease in tax credits

- decrease in quality of life as you spend more time earning and less time with family or doing the things you love

- Not to mention the increase in child care, meals, auto expenses, etc., leaving you pennies on the dollar in return, if any

Many people have realized that owning a home-based business is a better and more efficient solution to both these problems. Now, I know what you are thinking: "I don't know how to start a business. I don't have the money to get started in a business. I don't have time to start a business." But that is not true. Let me show you a way to get started in business and to grow that business for yourself using money you are already making, without overpaying to the government.

Perhaps increasing income is not your problem and your biggest need is a lower tax burden. I am going to share with you a way to fix that as well. Most people have no idea that saving $10,000 in taxes could actually mean more than increasing your income by $16,000. A penny saved is more than a penny earned.

Taxes are our greatest expense. We pay more in taxes than we pay in food, housing, transportation, and clothing combined. Because of this, lowering your taxes can be the greatest and quickest way to build wealth. You have to focus on lowering taxes as much as legally possible if you want to get ahead.

Did you know that by age 65, 96 percent of Americans are either dead, dead broke, or are supported by their family or the government.

Maybe preparing for the future is your concern. Did you know that by age 65, 96 percent of Americans are either dead, dead broke, or are supported by their family or the government. That shouldn't be. Working for an entire life can, and should, produce enough to secure your future. Let me help you do that!

Let's talk the IRS. You need to understand that in our country there are two types of tax systems: one for the W2 employee and one for the Business Owner (home-based business owner). Business owner taxes designed to allow a company to use its assets to invest in its own growth. They are given more opportunities for deductions and expenses, aka less taxes because a strong business is good for the economy as a whole, including the government. Individual (W2) taxes are designed to pay for the services the government provides, therefore, you're not getting any breaks. Business owner tax laws are designed to create wealth opportunity for growth, while the W2 tax laws limit your ability to grow. Because of the decrease in W2 deductions available with the 2018 tax code, it becomes crucial to have a business to reduce your tax burden.

Why does the government allow this? The number one reason is jobs; small businesses create 70 percent of job growth in our country. That is why businesses and the self-employed are allowed such huge tax deductions.

Congress knows that small businesses grow to one day to become Apple, Walmart, Costco, and Dollar General.

Let me share an example: Alexis is a W2 employee and has all the same bills we do (cell phone, mortgage or rent, utilities, car expenses, medical expenses, meals, and other miscellaneous expenses). She has to pay for all of these expenses using the money she has left over after she pays her taxes, what we call "after tax dollars." If Alexis started her own business, portions of these expenses that she is already spending are now redirected into business expenses and become deductible from her ordinary taxable income. The government allows you to use your losses against any form of income or you can carry forward those losses forever. If Alexis earns $60,000 per year as a W2 employee and she generates a loss of $15,000 for her business, she would only pay taxes on $45,000.

If you do not have a business, after what you've just heard, then you are brain dead. Just kidding! However, you are limiting your ability to take advantage of tax deductions and grow your wealth. If you're worried about how to fit owning a business into your schedule, don't be. There are no hourly requirements to owning a home-based business. If you are willing to spend forty-five minutes three to five days a week doing money-making activities, then you are entitled to deductions for a business. You can work your business part-time or full-time. You do not have to make a certain amount of income to qualify as a home-based business. However, you must attempt to make an income and you must run your business like a legitimate business, not a hobby.

I hope this has shown you how owning a home-based

business can drastically alter your financial situation, both in income and tax relief with little time commitment. Why not find a business that you are passionate about and use that passion to change your financial outlook?

Another reason to have a home-based business is it allows you to redirect your current living expenses into business expenses. Living expenses are day-to-day expenses such as your mortgage payment or rent, utility bills, meals, mileage, cell phone. Those are personal expenses, but they are also considered business expenses if you own your own business—allowing some massive tax savings on the money you're already spending. I have found that the average home-based business will increase your tax deductions and your take-home income by $4,000 to $8,000 per year if you just attempt income in a direct sales company or home-based business.

My suggestion is to find a home-based business or direct sales company in which you are passionate about their products and share those products with friends and family, allowing you to attempt to earn an income per the IRS. Not only could you make an extra stream of income, you can also decrease your tax burden at the same time. Decreasing taxes is truly the fastest way to wealth.

CHAPTER 11

Becoming a Trader Versus an Investor

Many people do not realize this, but you can actually be considered to be in business for yourself if you are a trader. Unlike being an investor (when someone else invests your money for you), you are trading your own money. When you are an investor, there is a major disadvantage, which is that you either have no deduction for expenses or there are phaseouts of deductions that would be allowed. There are also capital loss limitations to the amount of money that you make. For example, if you made $10,000 and lost $50,000, you could only claim $10,000. Also, with the 2018 new tax laws, it is questionable whether there will even be a way to claim these losses as the Schedule A miscellaneous deductions have been omitted from the tax code.

If you have a traditional business there are certain things that are not tax deductible for you that you can benefit from by having a second business that is home-based. Some of the biggest include commuting miles to and from your location and business use of your home. Meals with your friends can also be written off if you are sharing with them your product or service, so there is always a great reason to have another business. Find one that you are passionate about today and start sharing it for more income, tax deductions and to just simply help more people.

Trading, however, works completely different. The major advantage to being a trader is that all gains from the sale of stock, bonds, options, and currency are treated as capital gains and losses. They would usually end up being short-term in duration. Also, traders are allowed to treat all of their investment expenses as business expenses and not as itemized deductions, which is a huge deal. Traders can deduct conventions, continuing education, travel, and more when these things are related to your trading business. Also, all other investment expenses are deductible, with no thresholds, and any other reasonable business expenses are tax deductible, as well as you are considered to be in business if you are a trader. *Example*: Larry made $10,000 in gains as a trader and had $3,000 in losses. The $10,000 is a short-term capital gain and the $3,000 is completely deductible on the Schedule C, dollar for dollar. One of the biggest advantages is that a trader is not subject to social security taxes, unlike most traditional businesses.

So, what is a trader? First, traders must trade on a frequent basis throughout the year. They do not have to trade daily, but the more they trade, the better they look in the eyes of the IRS. The transactions should continue throughout the year and not just for a short period of time. Also, most of the gains should be short-term in nature, as traders are trading regularly, and should not consist of a substantial amount of dividends, interest, and long-term gains. Traders must have complete control over their investing and not allow someone else to handle or manage their money.

What are deductible expenses for a trader? Anything you can legitimately write off for a business, you can write off as a trader. One of the biggest tax advantages of trading is the fact that income is considered capital gains instead of ordinary income. Not having to pay the self-employment taxes of 15.3 percent is huge. Long-term gains are even less; depending on income, it could be as little as 0 percent and as much as 20 percent.

CHAPTER 12

Social Business:
A Life of Significance
By Sam Caster

I want to first share with you why this is the best chapter in my book. One year ago I was able to make a shift in my thinking and my business, and I realized that I am what Tony Robbins calls an artist. That means that I just really love what I do and have a passion to help people and make my craft better. That craft so happens to be accounting and tax strategy for small- to medium-sized businesses.

One year ago the shift happened because I attended an event that Tony Robbins was at, and I realized the gift I had was unlike any other accountant I had ever met. I realized my gift came to me through the school of hard knocks. Because I had failed in business and succeeded in different types of business, my skill set was completely different than that of a typical accountant. I am first and foremost an entrepreneur, and I have learned through business more about accounting than I think I ever would have sitting in a cubicle at an accounting firm. From owning my own businesses, I have sought to find ways to not only make my business more profitable, but also to gain more tax deductions. This process has not only helped me drastically, I have also been able to use the same information for my clients. Tony Robbins gave me the confidence in myself that I needed to be able to turn around my failures and start offering CFO services, consulting services and tax strategy sessions to help business owners not only make more but *save* more in taxes.

That is when my passion for accounting actually came to light. I started loving what I did and it really started showing to my clients. The funny thing is that I was giving them the advice all along, but because I was not charging for it, they were not really listening to me. That all changed in June 2017 when I had the major shift in my thinking. I realized that if you help more people get what they want, *I realized that if you help more people get what they want, you will automatically get what you want, as Zig Ziglar states.* you will automatically get what you want, as Zig Ziglar states. These are words to live by. Through my search to not only find great tax deductions but also improve my health and wealth, I was introduced to a company that allowed me to get healthy, lose weight, make some extra money, and have more tax deductions.

I was also introduced to a concept called Social Business, which completely transformed my way of thinking. It made me want to strive to not only be better for myself but to also strive for a much bigger purpose than simply my own. I did not fully understand the concept at first, and I really thought it was a sales tactic from this company to sell more products. When I truly started to get involved in the process and realized what a difference I was making, it caused me to make another shift. My purpose went from providing for my family and myself and helping clients to also working to eradicate childhood malnutrition.

I was also able to meet one of the most amazing men I have ever met. His name is Sam Caster and he is the founder of MannaRelief. In the rest of the chapter, you will hear his story and why he created the first ever Social Business 3.0. Now, I am not telling you that you need to partner with MannaRelief. What I am saying is that I have partnered with them because I love their purpose. Also, the fact that I am giving based upon my gross income from my business allows me to write off 100 percent of the proceeds given to MannaRelief as a Cost of Goods Sold.

I would suggest that you find something you are passionate about and give to that cause. When your passion and profits meet, it will create something inside you like nothing else can. God has truly blessed our family since we started giving to MannaRelief on April 15, 2018. We are now feeding on average 40,000 servings of nutrition to children in need, and there is nothing else like that feeling—knowing that because of our business and that decision, not only are we helping our clients and providing for ourselves, we are feeding more than 1,300 children a month.

The rest of this chapter is Sam Caster's story.

I have been an entrepreneur all my life. It is my skill, my gifting. My passion, on the other hand, is helping to meet the needs of the world's most vulnerable children. I heard a speaker say once that convergence in life occurs when you can combine what you are good at doing with what you are passionate about doing and find a way to monetize both. This describes a new breed of entrepreneur, called social entrepreneurs, and they are engaged in what is called Social Business.

Convergence in life occurs when you can combine what you are good at doing with what you are passionate about doing and find a way to monetize both.

Social Business combines the technology and profits of the for-profit industry with the heart, passion, and mission of the not-for-profit sector to provide sustainable solutions to the world's biggest problems. What distinguishes Social Business from traditional corporate giving is that it is a top line commitment versus charitable giving as a by-product of profitability. The social entrepreneur builds giving into the very fabric of his or her company's existence. Profits or no profits, a specific amount of giving is built into the cost of doing business.

In most companies, cause-based giving occurs as a result of profitability and only at levels that are comfortable for the company's balance sheet. There is nothing wrong with corporate giving; it is just not an absolute commitment to sustainable problem solving.

The most popular form of giving in a Social Business is called the Buy-One Give-One (BOGO) model. Tom's shoe company is the best known and most successful Social Business using this model of giving. Warby Parker eyeware, Soapbox cleaning products, and Bombas socks also have achieved success with BOGO. And while Social Business has become the most sought-after curriculum in business schools in countries around the world, my entrée into this exciting new arena was birthed from pure necessity.

MY STORY

I need to start with a bit of background to bring relevance to why I become a social entrepreneur. In 1993 I was introduced to a company that had discovered nature's most powerful immune modulating molecule in the fresh gel of the aloe vera plant. The company, Carrington Laboratories, at that time had received more than 130 worldwide patents on the processing and stabilization of this unique molecule with the objective of developing one of the world's first immunotherapeutic drugs for the treatment of a broad range of degenerate and autoimmune disorders.

The healing properties of this unique molecule are what established the aloe vera product as the cornerstone of ancient medicine in practically every culture on earth. But for some unknown reason, those dynamic healing properties completely disappeared when manufacturers began harvesting and processing aloe vera for use in a wide variety of consumer products in the 1960s. It did not keep the companies from proclaiming to have captured the "miracle" of aloe in their products, but the denaturing of this dynamic effect remained a mystery until the mid-1980s when a group of research pharmacologists from Southwestern Medical School was hired to solve the problem. They discovered that the immune effect was caused by a uniquely structured polysaccharide they named Acemannan.

Once the aloe leaf is picked, an enzyme is activated that begins to break down this molecule, and within twenty-four to forty-eight hours it completely loses its immune-activating quality. So, isolating and stabilizing Acemannan was the basis for many of their global patents. They succeeded in commercializing their discovery through the production of advanced wound care products and as both a vaccine adjustment and injectable immunostimulant for the treatment of tumors, cancer, and leukemia in veterinary medicine. But when Carrington petitioned the FDA for approval for human drug trials, it was rejected for a reason that seems absolutely mind-boggling. Because all drugs are toxic, phase one toxicity studies are mandated by the FDA before the drug can be used on humans. In phase one research, the investigative new drug is injected into laboratory mice at increasing dosages until an LD-50 is achieved; this is the lethal dose required to killed half the mice. That dosage is then used to determine the nonlethal dosage for humans. However, Acemannan had a major issue; it was completely nontoxic. Researchers could not make a mouse sick at any dose. Because, by law, all investigative new drugs must establish an LD-50, the application for phase II human trials was rejected in 1993.

At this point, I have to chalk this ridiculous rejection up to divine intervention because it set up the following series of events that led to a Social Business solution for addressing the number one cause of disease, disability, and death in children around the world.

Divine Intervention

In 1993, when I was introduced to the doctors who had discovered and extensively researched Acemannan, my goal was to help determine how to best penetrate the human market outside of the drug paradigm. I was absolutely overwhelmed by the powerful impact this molecule had on human physiology, and one thing became crystal clear: Acemannan did not have a classic drug effect on the body. Drugs alter the processes and biomarkers of chronic disease in order to address specifically expressed symptoms like pain or inflammation and are used in an attempt to poison diseased cells, as in the case of chemotherapy. Acemannan had no direct altering effect on specific diseased cells or biomarkers. It simply supercharged the immune system's ability to do what it is programmed to do: defend the body against

In other words, supercharge the body's ability to heal itself.

foreign invaders, destroy diseased cells before they proliferate, and facilitate the repair of damaged cells, tissues, and organs. In other words, supercharge the body's ability to heal itself.

As an entrepreneur, the potential market for this unique technology seemed unlimited. In 1994, I licensed the exclusive rights to this patented technology for distribution as a dietary supplement, opened a new company to facilitate that distribution, and began the process of educating consumers. The impact was immediate and profound. Individuals who had been struggling with chronic health issues saw dramatic quality of life improvements by simply "rebooting" their immune systems. World-class athletes experienced faster recovery from their training, and this allowed them to improve their world-class times through the ability to train longer and more frequently. I made Acemannan recovery products that were endorsed by USA Track and Field and distributed them to our Olympic athletes. From the sickest of the sickest to the healthiest of the healthy, the response to Acemannan was overwhelming.

Our company growth tripled several years in a row, and in 1999 the company went public to raise money for a massive international expansion. In 2005, *Businessweek* magazine ranked us as the sixth-best small company (under $1 billion in annual revenue) in America.

At this point of my life, I suppose I could have just been satisfied with the success I had achieved. It was the fulfillment of the entrepreneurial dream. But something happened along this journey that would change the direction of my life, career objectives, and goals forever.

I discovered my purpose. I heard a philosopher say once that humans strive through life to answer two questions: who am I, and why am I here? I had never thought much about purpose, because as an entrepreneur, I had focused almost all my efforts on creating and building a successful business.

My wife Linda and I are strong people of faith, and we knew that God had given us a heart for fatherless and vulnerable children. We have been blessed with five adopted children, and they are the true center of our universe. But in 1997, that passion for children was about to also transfer into a driving force in my career. We had been financially supporting an orphanage organization in Romania, and one of their caregivers had come to thank their contributors and give us an accountability of our donations. At the end of her talk, the caregiver said it was heartbreaking to see the suffering of the children, who without access to good food or medicine were susceptible to every form of poor health. Their orphans were constantly sick; they were losing thirty to forty children a year. The caregiver asked if we could help in any way.

The Epiphany

The minute I heard that plea, something inside me ignited. Poor nutrition is the number one cause of immunodeficiency in children, and once their immune systems are compromised, their bodies become breeding grounds for chronic and infectious disease. More than 6 million children die every year worldwide as a result of immunodeficiency-related issues. So, there I was, building a thriving business with nature's most powerful immune supporting technology, and I knew I could make a major impact in the lives of those children.

After the meeting, I introduced myself to the caregiver and informed her of the potential life-changing health benefits I could offer her children through the intervention of Acemannan. She was so excited when I agreed to donate a year's supply to their organization. All they had to do was mix it in whatever kind of meal they were able to provide. At the end of the year she reported that their children's health had dramatically improved and that, for the first time in a decade, not one child from their organization died, after losing forty per year in prior years. My heart jumped for joy, because for the first time in my life I realized what I was good at doing could be directly linked to what I was passionate about doing (i.e., convergence). The caregiver added that not only did they want more Acemannan, every other organization they were networked with around the world wanted to know how they too could get access to this amazing technology.

It did not take long for me to determine that charitable giving is not a sustainable model for nourishing children on a daily basis, but it was the only option we had.

To help facilitate this enormous demand, Linda and I founded our own not-for-profit called MannaRelief and began soliciting donors to help fund our mission. It did not take long for me to determine that charitable giving is not a sustainable model for nourishing children on a daily basis, but it was the only option we had. Linda and I were MannaRelief's biggest donors, but over the next several years our monthly donations grew to the level of nourishing between 50,000 and 60,000 children a day.

Then, in 2006, the economy took a nosedive, and we lost about 60 percent of our donors in less than six months. That meant we had to cut off the supply of Acemannan to more than 30,000 children a day. It did not take long before we got flooded with letters, texts, and emails from caregivers around the world pleading for help: "We know you're struggling, but you can't cut us off. Our children are getting sick again and reverting back to the same poor health conditions they had been experiencing before they had access to Acemannan." This was heartbreaking. My prayer became: "God, you know my passion for this project, and you've even blessed me with the best technology to impact these children's lives, but I don't know how to generate sustainable funding."

The answer to my prayer came a few months later when someone sent me an article from *Harvard Business Review*. It was titled, "Can Entrepreneurs Save the World?" It was all about a revolutionary new business model called Social Business and how social entrepreneurs were popping up all over the world, linking their new business ideas for bringing sustainable change to problems in their communities, their countries, and the world.

As I researched Social Business, I discovered a few keys to success:

1. Identify a problem no one else is effectively dealing with.

2. Create an innovative and often disruptive solution to that problem. (Change is often violently opposed when there are large profits in protecting status quo.)

3. Incorporate a Buy-One Give-One model of corporate giving. (It is the best way to link your consumer directly with the solution being provided.)

4. Own the exclusive rights to your product. (That gives you the best opportunity for repeat customers, which helps ensure sustainability.)

5. Find creative ways to compensate those who want to help champion your cause, and they will drive your project to the ends of the earth. (David Bornstein, author of *Social Entrepreneurship: What Everyone Needs to Know,* describes this as Social Business 3.0: entrepreneurs who build platforms that allow more people to participate and profit from Social Business by building teams and teams of teams to facilitate the rapid circulation of strategies that can change the world.)

My Defining Moment

Social Business was my answer to prayer. I had just one major obstacle. I had taken my for-profit business public, which meant that our board

Aggressive giving and increasing shareholder equity do not live on the same planet.

of directors was obligated to one main purpose: increasing shareholder equity. Aggressive giving and increasing shareholder equity do not live on the same planet. Fulfilling the destiny we felt called to through this new model of Social Business would require that I resign from the company we had successfully built over the last twenty years, give up the majority of our assets and income, and start all over again. Wow! Our lives would change dramatically, but the reward of saving the lives of millions of children completely outweighed the sacrifices we would have to make.

It took a few years to find all the right ingredients, which included a second generation Acemannan technology that had four to five times the immune-activating fractions of Acemannan per gram than our original product. The developer of this advanced Acemannan technology, Dr. Santiago Rodriguez, donated the exclusive rights to this new composition, named Immun, to our new project. I then linked MannaRelief with a company whose owners were ready and willing to transform their company into the world's first 3.0 Social Business.

In just the first six months of launching our BOGO strategy, we provided more than seven million servings of Acemannan to medically fragile and at-risk children around the world. That is more servings than were donated in the first seven years of MannaRelief, using the charitable funding model. And we haven't even started! For anyone who wants more purpose in their life, Social Business could be the answer to their prayers.

Note: Today, other companies and service providers are beginning to link their product sales and services to

MannaRelief. The author of this book, Courtney Epps, is one of the first to do so. Her business has become enormously blessed, and Linda and I thank her for allowing us to share our story and for her support of this amazing mission.

Note from Courtney: At the time of this book's publishing, MannaRelief has provided more than 106 million servings of food to children in need in ninety different countries and given needed nutrition to more than ten thousand medically fragile children, which helps their bodies fight sickness and disease, and heal, in dramatic ways. OTB Tax, my company, has contributed more than 300,000 servings of food to children in need through MannaRelief since starting our Social Business April 15, 2018. To find out more about how you can become a social entrepreneur and help us feed more children, or to work with a nonprofit you are passionate about, contact us today. We want to help you save more money so you can give more.

CHAPTER 13

Audit-Proofing Your Business

Does the word *audit* make you break out in a nervous sweat? That's OK. I will guide you through every step of how to get through this and make sure you are audit-proofing your books. You must understand first that being selected to be audited does not mean that the IRS or Department of Revenue believes you have done something wrong. Also, if you are a business owner, you have a 73 percent likelihood that you will be audited at least one time in a twenty-year period, according to tax attorney and CPA Sandy Botkin. Thankfully, I have only had a couple of clients audited during my eighteen years in accounting.

But I have helped handle numerous others, including one that lasted for seven days. I learned a lot in the room with that auditor, and what they were actually looking for, so I can in turn now share that with my clients. The first thing the auditor asked my client was: "What would it cost you to replace yourself?" My client immediately said, "Well, at least $60,000 a year." Next, the auditor asked her to determine if she was paying herself a reasonable salary. I stress this: *never answer this question.* Especially if you have not been paying yourself at all. Once she said $60,000, my client was going to get hit with 25 percent for not paying herself a paycheck, and then she would have to pay self-employment of 15.3 percent, and federal and state, which is another 29 percent (in her situation). That is an extra $41,000 in taxes. I had advised my client not to answer any questions before I arrived, and that one question was going to cost her $41,000, times two, as her 2013 and 2014 returns were being audited.

I ended up working with the auditor and explaining that my client does not work in the business on a day-to-day basis, that what she does consists of ten to fifteen hours per week, and that someone could be paid ten dollars an hour to do the same work. We derived a yearly income of $18,000, which was only $12,400 in taxes. *Huge difference.* So, make sure you have a competent accountant who is working with you through your audit and that the accountant is going to be there to answer all questions. I am not telling you to lie—by no means am I saying that—but there are things in the tax code that you may not understand, and you would be much better off allowing an accountant to handle those issues than yourself. Do not give more information than you have been asked, either.

The most important thing to understand about an audit is that you do not want to ignore the audit! This will make you look as if you're trying to hide something.

All interviews for audits are going to be in person. You will receive paperwork in the mail that you are required to respond to and provide documentation for. If you do not have everything that they are requesting, don't panic! There are certain parts of the tax code that we help you with if you don't have receipts under seventy-five dollars, but be sure to provide everything you have that is requested of you. This could include mileage logs, receipts, general ledgers, P&L statements, and balance sheets.

Also, you want to make sure the IRS has your correct address in the event that you move. This could cause a major issue if you are audited and do not receive the audit request documents. This happened to me, as I had moved. I had no clue that my tax return was being audited, and the paperwork was not forwarded to me. It took me three and a half years to resolve this matter; I had to request to reopen the audit, then appeal the audit, and finally the IRS released my $23,000 refund (they had taken my refund every year for three years). To change your address, you will need to fill out an 8822 form, which is a change of address form. Not filling out this form will cost you a lot of time and more effort on your part, since the paperwork will not get to you, and you will have to track it down from the IRS or state agencies. It could also cause your refund to be held up. It could take up to nine months for the IRS to release a new check for your refund.

It is imperative that you send your tax return electronically. This will not only get you your refund faster, it's proof that your tax return has been filed. You want to make sure you have a competent tax preparer doing your taxes. It definitely helps if you are audited to have someone to rely on instead of yourself. A tax software will not go to an audit for you! It is important as well that your tax preparer is available year-round for you to ask questions and help with tax matters as the issues usually come up long after tax season is over!

I would advise that you not do your own tax returns; the IRS realizes that you are more likely to create errors than a tax professional, and that could increase your chances of being audited. Also, one tax strategy session with a competent accountant will enlighten you, likely, on thousands of dollars that you are not taking in tax deductions. I have had clients miss $50,000 in expenses in one year by trying to put together their own P&Ls for a tax preparer. *What you do not know will cost you.* If you are given expert advice on a particular deduction or item, please make sure that you keep a record of that item, because if that advice is found to be incorrect, having the record could save you penalties and interest.

You should never brag to anyone that you have not paid taxes or filed your returns. There may be a legitimate reason behind both of these, but you must know that the failure to file a tax return when you owe money is considered tax evasion and is illegal. If someone gets angry with you and decides to contact the IRS, there is—believe this or not—a 30 percent finder's fee for people who turn you in. (You can find this information in IRS Publication 733.) The most common occurrences of people who turn people in include angry ex-boyfriends or ex-girlfriends, ex-spouses, and ex-employees. Watch what you say, because it can be used against you.

The IRS has implemented numerous sophisticated software programs to find people who don't report all of their income. Don't try to hide your income from them. This is illegal. Not paying all that you owe, however, is tax avoidance. Although frowned upon, it is not illegal.

There are a couple of myths I would like to address about audits. One is that you are more likely to be audited if you take certain deductions, such as business use of your home or car expenses. This is not true, and if you are entitled to the deductions, you should take them! There is no reason for you to give the government more money than it is entitled to receive. What can potentially trigger an audit is if your income drastically increases or decreases.

Another myth is that audits are done immediately. It usually takes two years before you receive anything from the IRS in reference to an audit or similar issues that are taking place. Another myth is that professionally filed returns are audit-proof. This is just not true, but taking this step definitely does help eliminate errors that could cause you to be audited. Again, it is best to e-file your return, and it is always a great idea to have an accountant prepare your return.

Another myth is that you should be extremely afraid of an audit. This is just not true. (Though, understand, I am not saying audits are fun.) Understand that an audit is just to determine that the information on your return can be proven. The biggest reason people lose on audits is because they don't have the receipts or backup to prove their expenses. Auditors like backup. I've also found that you have a much better chance if you have an accounting software such as Quickbooks so that you can provide the auditor with a general ledger, P&L, and balance sheet that ties back to your tax return.

If You Are Audited

One of the most important things to understand is that you need to assume you are going to be audited when you prepare your tax return. You need to keep six years' worth of data and be able to easily find and explain that information to an auditor. If you simply keep the documents with your tax return records from year to year, it makes things much easier if you are selected to be audited.

You want to make sure that you do not, in any way, try to avoid an auditor. You will make the auditor believe you are hiding something, and then they may become overly zealous trying to find something that you could be leaving out.

You have not done anything wrong if you are audited. It simply means that the government is requesting more information. You want to make sure that you only bring the information that is requested by the auditor, because you do not want to trigger a red flag on something else that the auditor is not looking for. You also must understand that you have to prove your deductions are valid. The IRS does not have to prove anything, and this is where it becomes crucial to keep a good accounting of all your deductions. You should be prepared to answer questions, and it's an excellent idea to have a competent accountant do this for you. Make sure that you are organized, as your auditor is going to think that your return doesn't have sufficient backup if you are disorganized, and that will, once again, start a fishing expedition. This can result in more in-depth audits or going back prior years for auditing. The more organized you are, the faster your audit is going to be. You do not want to volunteer information.

If you disagree with the auditor, do not argue with him or her. If you think you are right, however, ask the auditor or agent for the legal reference. Do not accept vague statements as interpretations of the law. Tell them, "My accountant told me that this deduction is proper. Can you give me something to show that he's wrong?" However, do not, in any manner, get in an argument with an auditor. If you have an issue that you cannot resolve, ask for their supervisor's contact information.

Last, you should never tamper with evidence or lie to an agent. This is a federal offense. Understand as well that your accountant has no privilege protecting your communication on criminal matters. Any communication with your accountant can be obtained by the IRS in a criminal matter. And you *never* want to be alone with a special agent. These people are not "special" in any way. Their one and only job is to investigate criminal activities. You will want to seek a criminal tax attorney, immediately, to help with this matter. If you do decide to talk, understand that it is easier for the government to prove that you are lying to a federal official than it is to get you on the crime itself!

A few more things you want to be aware of if you are audited: you should dress normally, and be on time for the audit. Auditors don't like people who act and look as if they have no money, and, in the same way, they don't like people who act and look like they have more money than they do. Just be normal; be yourself. Auditors are graded on their efficiency. If you are late for your appointment and cause the auditor to be inefficient in what he or she is doing, you are definitely starting off on the wrong foot. If you are late, it gives the auditor more time to examine your return and see if they can find any issues.

You do not, in any way, want to give in too quickly. Auditors will believe you are trying to hide something if you agree to adjustments too quickly. The IRS may actually look *further* into deductions if you seem too eager to end an audit.

You have many rights as a taxpayer, and you should know those rights. Make sure you are as aggressive with your deductions as possible, but also make sure you have your backup information if you are audited.

Also, statistics show you are two to twenty times more likely to be audited if you have a Schedule C business as opposed to an LLC treated as an S Corporation. This is still one more reason to have an S Corporation.

DEDUCTIONS
(* – REQUIRES PLAN)

Accounting fees
Advertising
All necessary business expenses
Amortization
Annual meetings
Attorney fees
Auto expenses
Bad debts
Banking fees
Board meetings
Building repairs and maintenance
Cafeteria plan*
Casualty damages
Charitable deductions*
Child care*
Cleaning/janitorial
Collection expenses
Commissions to outside parties
Computers and tech supplies
Consulting fees
Continuing education
Conventions and trade shows
Cost of goods sold
Depletion
Depreciation
Dining expenses
Discounts to customers
Embezzlement losses
Payroll for family
Employee retirement plans
Freight or shipping costs

Furniture and fixtures
Subcontractors
Health insurance
Home office
Internet hosting and services
Interest
License fees
Investment advice and fees
Laundry while traveling
Lobbying (if qualifying)
Magazines
Maintenance education asst.*
Management fees
Materials dues (professional club)
Medical expenses*
Membership dues
Moving equipment toyalties
Newspapers exhibits for publicity
Safe deposit box
Office supplies and expenses
Outside services
Payroll taxes
Parking gifts (limits apply)
Pension
Periodicals
Group insurance (if qualifying)
Postage
Prizes for contests
Publicity
Real estate-related
Rebates on sales

Rent

Repairs

Storage rentals

Research and development

Property taxes

Franchise taxes

Sales tax

Theft

Travel

Unemployment compensation

Utilities

Website design

Workers compensation

BUSINESS USE OF HOME

(BASED ON PERCENTAGE OF USE)

Mortgage interest or rent

HOA fees

Utilities

Repairs and maintenance

Homeowners insurance

Real estate property taxes

Alarm system

Depreciation of home

Depreciation of furniture and equipment

ENDNOTES

1. Warren Buffett Says: 'Always Have 2 Sources of Income' – Why and How to Do It." *Warren Buffett,* Wikiquote, 21 Oct. 2018, 15:32, en.wikiquote.org/wiki/Warren_Buffett.

2. Botkin, Sanford C., *Lower Your Taxes—Big Time!: Wealth-Building, Tax Reduction Secrets from an IRS Insider,* 2016-2017 edition (McGraw-Hill Education, 2017).

3. Ibid.

Information in this book is also taken from these sources:

Botkin, Sanford C., *Seven Simple Ways to Legally Avoid Paying Taxes* (Taxbot LLC, 2018).

Kiyosaki, Robert T., *Rich Dads Retire Young, Retire Rich: How to Get Rich Quickly and Stay Rich Forever* (Warner Books, 2012).

Kohler, Mark J., *What Your CPA Isn't Telling You: Life-Changing Tax Strategies* (Entrepreneur Media Inc., 2011).

"10 Commonly Overlooked Tax Breaks for the Self-Employed," Quickbooks, 2018, quickbooks.intuit.com/r/taxes/10-commonly-overlooked-tax-breaks-for-the-self-employed/.

A great deal of information in this book is taken from the Internal Revenue Code. Various sections cited. These are carefully listed throughout.

ABOUT THE AUTHOR

COURTNEY EPPS is the wife of Brandon Epps and the proud mother of six children. The family lives in Greenville, S.C. She has more than eighteen years of experience in the accounting and finance industry. She is a Fractional CFO to more than a dozen small- to medium-sized companies and owns a full-service accounting firm, Outside the Box Business Solutions, LLC. She has owned her business for seventeen years. Her experience is in public and cost accounting, providing clients with tax preparation, tax planning, income tax accounting, and consulting services to better run a business. With years of experience, she has developed advanced technical skills in a wide variety of tax and accounting areas and has served clients from start-up businesses to multi-million-dollar companies. Courtney has worked with companies that span a range of industries and sizes. She has developed a broad expertise of industries including trucking, doctor's offices, real estate, construction, convention companies, and others, as well as home-based and network marketing businesses.